VOCABULARY HANDBOOK

CORE LITERACY LIBRARY

Vocabulary Handbook

Linda Diamond

Linda Gutlohn

·P A U L·H·
BROOKES
PUBLISHING Cº ®

BALTIMORE • LONDON • SYDNEY

CORE   OAKLAND, CALIFORNIA

Paul H. Brookes Publishing Co.
Post Office Box 10624
Baltimore, Maryland 21285-0624

Consortium on Reaching Excellence in Education, Inc. (CORE)
1300 Clay Street, Suite 600
Oakland, California 94612

For information about Consortium on Reaching Excellence in Education, Inc., and professional development related
to this content or other literacy topics, please call toll-free 1-888-249-6155 or visit www.corelearn.com.

This edition of *Vocabulary Handbook* is co-produced and published jointly by Consortium on Reaching
Excellence in Education, Inc. and Paul H. Brookes Publishing Co., Inc. and was manufactured in the
United States of America.

Fourteeth printing, September 2021.

ORDERING INFORMATION

To order *Vocabulary Handbook,* please call Paul H. Brookes Publishing Co., 1-410-337-9580
or toll-free 1-800-638-3775, or visit www.brookespublishing.com.

CREDITS

Editorial Director: Linda Gutlohn
Book Design and Production: Lucy Nielsen
Editorial: Susan Blackaby, Lawrence DiStasi, Shelle Epton, Tom Hassett, Michael Seifert, David Sweet
Manufacturing Consultant: Kyrill Schabert
Special acknowledgment is given to James Baumann, Isabel Beck, Andrew Biemiller, and Michael F. Graves for their
contributions to vocabulary research.

Library of Congress Cataloging-in-Publication Data

Diamond, Linda, 1949–
    Vocabulary handbook / Linda Diamond, Linda Gutlohn.
        p.   cm. — (Core literacy library)
    Includes bibliographical references and index.
    ISBN-13: 978-1-55766-928-5 (pbk.)
    ISBN-10: 1-55766-928-7 (pbk.)
    1. Vocabulary—Study and teaching—Handbooks, manuals, etc. I. Gutlohn, Linda. II. Title.
    LB1574.5.D53 2007
    372.44—DC22   2006100049

British Library Cataloguing in Publication data are available from the British Library.

CONTENTS

Chapter 2: Word-Learning Strategies

Chapter 3: Word Consciousness

For educators at every level, the *Vocabulary Handbook* is a comprehensive reference about vocabulary instruction. Organized according to the elements of explicit instruction (what? why? when? and how?), the handbook includes both a research-informed knowledge base and practical sample lesson models.

what?

a thorough but concise graphic explanation of research-based content and practices

why?

a readable summary of scientifically based research, selected quotes from researchers, and a bibliography of suggested reading

when?

information about instructional sequence, assessment and intervention strategies, and standardized vocabulary tests

how?

sample lesson models providing a bridge between research and practice, and making explicit instruction easy

The *Vocabulary Handbook* combines the best features of an academic text and a practical hands-on teacher's guide. Starting with the introduction, each chapter of the handbook examines a component of effective vocabulary instruction.

WHAT? · WHY? · WHEN? · HOW?

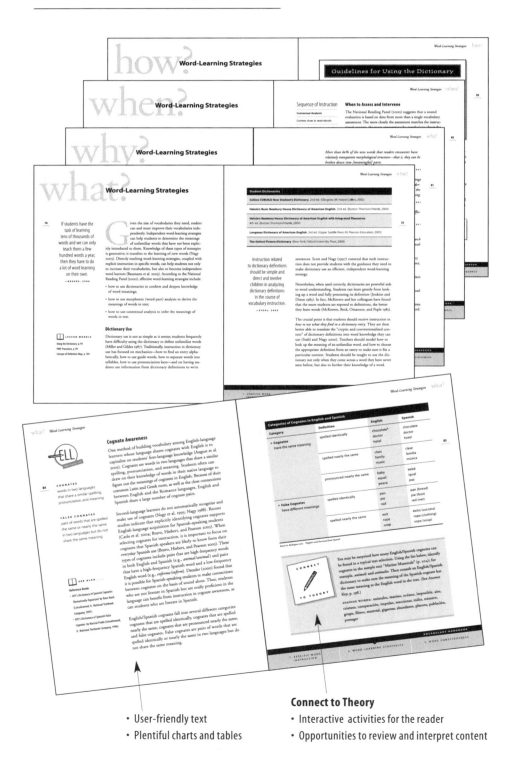

• User-friendly text
• Plentiful charts and tables

Connect to Theory

• Interactive activities for the reader
• Opportunities to review and interpret content

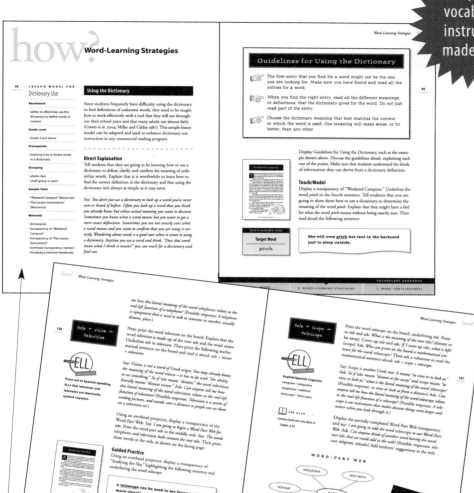

Explicit vocabulary instruction made easy!

Lesson Model Features

- Focus and materials sidebar
- Explicit instruction
- Clear explanation
- Teacher modeling
- Useful background information
- Identification of research base
- Support for English-language learners
- Easy-to-follow "teacher's guide" format

RESOURCES

The Resources section provides reproducible sample texts, activity masters, and teaching charts designed to be used in conjunction with sample lesson models. Sample texts include narrative and informational texts that provide a context for explicit instruction.

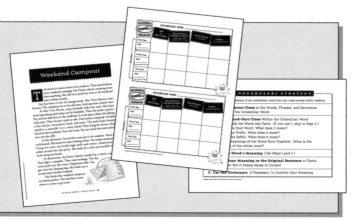

The Handbook can be used by . . .

- **elementary teachers**
  to enhance vocabulary instruction in core reading programs

- **middle and high school teachers**
  to enhance language arts and content-area instruction

- **college professors and students**
  as a textbook for pre-service teacher education

- **providers of professional development**
  as an educational tool

- **school or district administrators**
  to support and facilitate effective instruction

- **literacy coaches**
  as a resource for implementation

- **teachers of English-language learners (ELLs)**
  to support in-depth vocabulary acquisition

- **teachers of struggling readers**
  to help build word knowledge in students with impoverished vocabularies

VOCABULARY HANDBOOK

Introduction

specific
word
instruction
word-learning
strategies word
consciousness

Introduction

VOCABULARY
knowledge of words and word meanings

Vocabulary is the knowledge of words and word meanings. As Steven Stahl (2005) puts it, "Vocabulary knowledge is knowledge; the knowledge of a word not only implies a definition, but also implies how that word fits into the world." Vocabulary knowledge is not something that can ever be fully mastered; it is something that expands and deepens over the course of a lifetime.

Instruction in vocabulary involves far more than looking up words in a dictionary and using the words in a sentence. Vocabulary is acquired incidentally through indirect exposure to words and intentionally through explicit instruction in specific words and word-learning strategies. According to Michael Graves (2000), there are four components of an effective vocabulary program: (1) wide or extensive independent reading to expand word knowledge, (2) instruction in specific words to enhance comprehension of texts containing those words, (3) instruction in independent word-learning strategies, and (4) word consciousness and word-play activities to motivate and enhance learning. This handbook covers the last three components.

Components of Effective Vocabulary Instruction

Incidental Vocabulary Learning

Rich Oral Language Experiences

Wide Reading
Teacher Read-Alouds
Independent Reading

Intentional Vocabulary Teaching

Specific Word Instruction
Rich and Robust Instruction of Words in Text

Word-Learning Strategies
Dictionary Use
Morphemic Analysis
Contextual Analysis
Cognate Awareness (ELL)

Word Consciousness Adept Diction • Word Play • Word Origins

Vocabulary Forms		
	RECEPTIVE	**PRODUCTIVE**
ORAL	**Listening** words we understand when others speak or read aloud to us	**Speaking** words we use when we talk to others
PRINT	**Reading** words we understand when we read them	**Writing** words we use when we write

4

Individuals have various
types of vocabulary
that they use for
different purposes.

—KAMIL & HIEBERT, 2005

Forms of Vocabulary

There are various types, or forms, of vocabulary. Words themselves are encountered in two forms: oral and print. Oral vocabulary is the set of words for which students know the meanings when others speak or read aloud to them, or when they speak to others. Print vocabulary is the set of words for which students know the meanings when they read or write silently. In emergent readers, oral vocabulary is much larger than print vocabulary. As students become more literate, print vocabulary plays an increasingly larger role (Kamil and Hiebert 2005). Ultimately, print vocabulary is "much more extensive and diverse" than oral vocabulary (Hayes, Wolfer, and Wolfe 1996).

The knowledge of word meanings, or vocabulary, can also be divided according to whether it is receptive or productive. Receptive vocabulary is the set of words to which a student can assign some meaning when listening or reading. Productive vocabulary is the set of words students use frequently in their speaking and writing. Receptive vocabulary (listening or reading) is generally larger than productive vocabulary (speaking or writing) because people usually recognize more words than they regularly use.

> Word learning is
> incremental; that is,
> it proceeds in
> a series of steps.
>
> **—GRAVES &
> WATTS-TAFFE, 2002**

Extent of Word Knowledge

The extent of word knowledge has serious implications for how words are taught and how word knowledge is measured (Beck, McKeown, and Kucan 2002). According to Dale (1965), four levels can be used to describe the extent of a person's word knowledge: (1) have never seen or heard the word before, (2) have seen or heard the word before, but don't know what it means, (3) vaguely know the meaning of the word; can associate it with a concept or context, and (4) know the word well; can explain it and use it. As an unfamiliar word is encountered repeatedly over time, knowledge of the word grows and the word moves up the levels toward "know the word well." According to Graves and Watts-Taffe (2002), Dale's fourth level can be further divided into "having a full and precise meaning versus having a general meaning or using the word in writing versus only recognizing it when reading."

5

CONNECT TO THEORY

Using Dale's levels of word knowledge described above, analyze the extent of your knowledge about each of the words listed in the chart below.

LEVELS OF WORD KNOWLEDGE			
	1	**2**	**3**	**4**
affix				
context				
dyslexia				
fricative				
mnemonic				
prosody				

6

WORD FAMILY

a group of words related
in meaning.

88,500 distinct word families
in printed school English

40,000 word families known
by Grade 12

ROOT WORD

a single word that cannot
be broken into smaller words
or parts

17,500 root word meanings
in *The Living Word Vocabulary*
(Grades K–12)

15,000 root word meanings
known well by Grade 12

 **SEE ALSO . . .**

Root Words and Word Families, p. 77

Vocabulary Size

Estimates of student vocabulary size vary dramatically (Anderson and Freebody 1981). The variation occurs because of differences in the procedures used by vocabulary researchers and in the definition of what is counted as a distinct word (Anderson 1996). Researchers Nagy and Anderson (1984) and Biemiller (2005b) use different descriptive terms for what is counted as a distinct word.

Nagy and Anderson (1984) attempted to resolve questions about the size of the vocabulary-learning task. Using a corpus of words gathered from school materials and textbooks (Carroll, Davies, and Richman 1971), they grouped related words into families by judging whether a student who knew the meaning of only one of the words in a family could infer the meanings of other related words in the family. For example, *sweet, sweetness,* and *sweetly* belong to the same word family. Compound words were judged in a similar way. From this analysis, Nagy and Anderson estimated that there are about 88,500 distinct word families in printed school English, and that an average twelfth grader probably knows about 40,000 of them.

While Nagy and Anderson (1984) count occurrences of word families, Biemiller (2005b) counts occurrences of root words. But since one word family is equivalent to one root word (and its related forms), the approach is essentially the same for both. Biemiller believes that when the meaning of a root word is known, derived words (i.e., other words in the word family) and compound words can probably be largely inferred from context while reading. According to Biemiller (2004), in Dale and O'Rourke's *The Living Word Vocabulary* (1981) there are about 17,500 root words known by students in Grade 12. Of these root words, they estimate that about 15,000 words are known well by a majority of students.

> By the end of Grade 2, students know an average of about 6,000 root word meanings.
>
> — BIEMILLER, 2005a

How Many Root Words Are Acquired per Year?

According to Biemiller (2005a), children through Grade 6 typically acquire about 800 to 1,000 root-word meanings per year. From age 1 through Grade 2, children gain an average of 860 root words per year, or about 2.4 words per day. From Grades 3 to 6, they gain an average of 1,000 root words per year, or about 2.8 root words per day. Biemiller's estimates are based on the known number of root words at each level of *The Living Word Vocabulary* (Dale and O'Rourke 1981).

Average Number of Root Words Acquired by Average Students

Age or Grade	Per Year	Per Week	Per Day
Ages 1–4	860	16.5	2.4
Grades K–2	860	16.5	2.4
Grades 3–6	1,000	19.2	2.8

Based on Biemiller 2005a.

Estimates of Cumulative Root-Word Knowledge

Age or Grade	Average Number of Root Words
End of Age 1	860
End of Age 2	1,720
End of Age 3	2,580
End of Age 4 (Pre-K)	3,440
End of Age 5 (K)	4,300
End of Grade 1	5,160
End of Grade 2	6,020
End of Grade 3	7,020
End of Grade 4	8,020
End of Grade 5	9,020
End of Grade 6	10,020

Based on Biemiller 2005a.

How Many Derived Words Are Acquired per Year?

A study by Anglin (1993) indicates that in Grade 1 the number of derived words (i.e., affixed or compound words) that students acquire is three times the number of root words. By Grade 5, the number of derived words and idioms increases to five times the number of root words.

Ratio of Root Words Acquired to Derived Words Acquired per Year

Grade	Root Words	Ratio	Derived Words
Grade 1	860	860 x 3	2,580
Grade 5	1,000	1,000 x 5	5,000

Based on Biemiller 2005a; Anglin 1993.

How Many Words Can Be Taught Directly?

When it comes to the number of root words or word families that can be taught in a school year, vocabulary researchers are basically in agreement. About 2 words per day, or 10 per week, can be taught directly.

Average Number of Root Words or Word Families that Can Be Taught Directly

Per School Week	Per School Year/180 days	Researcher
about 10	360 root words	Biemiller 2005a
about 8 to 10	about 400 word families	Beck et al. 2002
about 8 to 10	300 to 400 word families	Stahl et al. 1986

The Vocabulary Gap

Profound differences exist in vocabulary knowledge among learners. The word knowledge gap between groups of children begins before children enter school. This gap is too often not closed in later years. Hart and Risley (1995) found, for example, that three-year-olds from advantaged homes had oral vocabularies as much as five times larger than children from disadvantaged homes. Without intervention, this gap grows ever larger as students proceed through school.

> Focusing vocabulary instruction on acquiring root words is an effective way to address the large number of words that students must learn each year.
>
> —BIEMILLER & SLONIM, 2001

Biemiller (2005a) estimates that the bottom 25 percent of students begin Kindergarten with 1,000 fewer root-word meanings than average students. To make matters worse, these students who have the smallest vocabularies acquire only about 1.6 root words per day as compared with average students, who acquire about 2.4 root words per day. By the end of Grade 2, this results in a difference of about 2,000 words between average students and lower-quartile students. In fact, the number of root words known by a second grader in the lowest vocabulary quartile is about the same as the number of root words known by an average Kindergartener (Anglin 1993; Biemiller and Slonim 2001; Biemiller 2005a).

9

**The Vocabulary Gap
in Root-Word Knowledge**

Grade	Average Student (at 2.4 root words per day)	Bottom 25% (at 1.6 root words per day)
End of Pre-K	3,440	2,440
End of K	4,300	3,016
End of Grade 1	5,160	3,592
End of Grade 2	6,020	4,168

To close the vocabulary gap in students who have impoverished vocabularies, vocabulary acquisition must be accelerated (Biemiller 2005b). According to Biemiller (2003, 2005a), "at the very least, it would seem desirable to prevent further decrements" by teaching at least two root-word meanings a day to students in Kindergarten through Grade 2. After Grade 2, all students, including those in the lowest quartile, apparently learn new root words at about the same rate (Biemiller and Slonim 2001). However, because of the initial vocabulary gap, if students in the lowest quartile are to ever "catch up" with their higher-level peers, they will need to learn words at an even faster rate—3.5 to 4 root words per school day (Biemiller 2003).

Vocabulary seems
to occupy an important
middle ground in
learning to read.

—NATIONAL READING
PANEL, 2000

10

Links Between Vocabulary and Comprehension

Vocabulary occupies an important position both in learning to read and in comprehending text: readers cannot understand text without knowing what most of the words mean (National Reading Panel 2000). According to Nagy (2005), "Of the many benefits of having a large vocabulary, none is more valuable than the positive contribution that vocabulary size makes to reading comprehension." To comprehend text, students require *both* fluent word recognition skills (i.e., decoding) and an average or greater vocabulary. According to Biemiller (2005b), "the presence of these two accomplishments does not guarantee a high level of reading comprehension, but the absence of *either* word recognition or adequate vocabulary ensures a low level of reading comprehension."

The Connecticut Longitudinal Study (Foorman et al. 1997) demonstrates that first-grade decoding ability (i.e., word recognition) is a major factor in reading comprehension, especially as students progress through the grades. Once a reader decodes a word, oral vocabulary plays a predominant part in reading comprehension. When beginning readers come to an unfamiliar word in text, they try to use the words they have heard—the words in their oral vocabularies—to make sense of the word in print. If the word is part of their oral vocabularies, readers can more easily and quickly decode and understand it (Kamil and Hiebert 2005).

For accomplished decoders, vocabulary knowledge probably plays more of a role in reading comprehension than word recognition skills (Biemiller 2005b). Cunningham and Stanovich (1997) found that first-grade orally tested vocabulary was predictive of eleventh-grade reading comprehension, whereas first-grade word recognition skills were not. From about third grade on, 95 percent of students can read more words than they can define or explain (Biemiller and Slonim 2001). The role of an early deficit in oral vocabulary thus becomes magnified.

Components of Vocabulary Instruction

The National Reading Panel (2000) concluded that there is no single research-based method for teaching vocabulary. From its analysis, the panel recommended using a variety of direct and indirect methods of vocabulary instruction.

Intentional Teaching

Specific Word Instruction

• Selecting Words to Teach
• Rich and Robust Instruction

Word-Learning Strategies

• Dictionary Use
• Morphemic Analysis
• Cognate Awareness (ELL)
• Contextual Analysis

 SEE ALSO . . .

Chapter 1: Specific Word Instruction

Chapter 2: Word-Learning Strategies

Intentional Vocabulary Teaching   11

According to the National Reading Panel (2000), explicit instruction of vocabulary is highly effective. To develop vocabulary intentionally, students should be explicitly taught both specific words and word-learning strategies. To deepen students' knowledge of word meanings, specific word instruction should be robust (Beck et al. 2002). Seeing vocabulary in rich contexts provided by authentic texts, rather than in isolated vocabulary drills, produces robust vocabulary learning (National Reading Panel 2000). Such instruction often does not begin with a definition, for the ability to give a definition is often the result of knowing what the word means. Rich and robust vocabulary instruction goes beyond definitional knowledge; it gets students actively engaged in using and thinking about word meanings and in creating relationships among words.

Research shows that there are more words to be learned than can be directly taught in even the most ambitious program of vocabulary instruction. Explicit instruction in word-learning strategies gives students tools for independently determining the meanings of unfamiliar words that have not been explicitly introduced in class. Since students encounter so many unfamiliar words in their reading, any help provided by such strategies can be useful.

Word-learning strategies include dictionary use, morphemic analysis, and contextual analysis. For ELLs whose language shares cognates with English, cognate awareness is also an important strategy. Dictionary use teaches students about multiple word

12

> When children "know"
> a word, they not
> only know the word's
> definition and its
> logical relationship
> with other words,
> they also know how the
> word functions
> in different contexts.
>
> — STAHL & KAPINUS, 2001

Word Consciousness

Adept Diction

Word Play

Word Histories and Origins

 SEE ALSO...

Chapter 3: Word Consciousness

meanings, as well as the importance of choosing the appropriate definition to fit the particular context. Morphemic analysis is the process of deriving a word's meaning by analyzing its meaningful parts, or morphemes. Such word parts include root words, prefixes, and suffixes. Contextual analysis involves inferring the meaning of an unfamiliar word by scrutinizing the text surrounding it. Instruction in contextual analysis generally involves teaching students to employ both generic and specific types of context clues.

Fostering Word Consciousness

A more general way to help students develop vocabulary is by fostering word consciousness, an awareness of and interest in words. Word consciousness is not an isolated component of vocabulary instruction; it needs to be taken into account each and every day (Scott and Nagy 2004). It can be developed at all times and in several ways: through encouraging adept diction, through word play, and through research on word origins or histories. According to Graves (2000), "If we can get students interested in playing with words and language, then we are at least halfway to the goal of creating the sort of word-conscious students who will make words a lifetime interest."

Multiple Exposures in Multiple Contexts

One principle of effective vocabulary learning is to provide multiple exposures to a word's meaning. There is great improvement in vocabulary when students encounter vocabulary words often (National Reading Panel 2000). According to Stahl (2005), students probably have to see a word more than once to place it firmly in their long-term memories. "This does *not* mean mere repetition or drill of the word," but seeing the word in different and multiple contexts. In other words, it is important that vocabulary instruction provide students with opportunities to encounter words repeatedly and in more than one context.

Findings of the National Reading Panel

Intentional instruction of vocabulary items is required for specific texts.

Repetition and multiple exposures to vocabulary items are important.

Learning in rich contexts is valuable for vocabulary learning.

Vocabulary tasks should be restructured as necessary.

Vocabulary learning should entail active engagement in learning tasks.

Computer technology can be used effectively to help teach vocabulary.

Vocabulary can be acquired through incidental learning.

How vocabulary is assessed and evaluated can have differential effects on instruction.

Dependence on a single vocabulary instructional method will not result in optimal learning.

Restructuring of Vocabulary Tasks

It is often assumed that when students do not learn new vocabulary words, they simply need to practice the words some more. Research has shown, however, that it is often the case that students simply do not understand the instructional task involved (National Reading Panel 2000). Rather than focus only on the words themselves, teachers should be certain that students fully understand the instructional tasks (Schwartz and Raphael 1985). The restructuring of learning materials or strategies in various ways often can lead to increased vocabulary acquisition, especially for low-achieving or at-risk students (National Reading Panel 2000). According to Kamil (2004), "once students know what is expected of them in a vocabulary task, they often learn rapidly."

13

Incidental Vocabulary Learning

The scientific research on vocabulary instruction reveals that most vocabulary is acquired incidentally through indirect exposure to words. Students can acquire vocabulary incidentally by engaging in rich oral-language experiences at home and at school, listening to books read aloud to them, and reading widely on their own. Reading volume is very important in terms of long-term vocabulary development (Cunningham and Stanovich 1998). Kamil and Hiebert (2005) reason that extensive reading gives students repeated or multiple exposures to words and is also one of the means by which students see vocabulary in rich contexts. Cunningham (2005) recommends providing structured read-aloud and discussion sessions and extending independent reading experiences outside school hours to encourage vocabulary growth in students.

Strategies for ELLs

Take Advantage of Students' First Language

Teach the Meaning of Basic Words

Review and Reinforcement

 SEE ALSO . . .

Selecting Words for English-Language
Learners (ELLs), p. 21
Word Tiers and Suggested Teaching
Methods for ELLs, p. 22
Cognate Awareness, p. 84
Categories of Cognates in English and
Spanish, p. 85

 LESSON MODELS

Introducing Function Words, p. 48
Vocabulary Hotshot Notebook, p. 189

Instruction for English-Language Learners (ELLs)

An increasing number of students come from homes in which English is not the primary language. From 1979 to 2003, the number of students who spoke English with difficulty increased by 124 percent (National Center for Education Statistics 2005). In 2003, students who spoke English with difficulty represented approximately 5 percent of the school population—up from 3 percent in 1979.

Not surprisingly, vocabulary development is especially important for English-language learners (ELLs). Poor vocabulary is a serious issue for these students (Calderón et al. 2005). ELLs who have deficits in their vocabulary are less able to comprehend text at grade level than their English-only (EO) peers (August et al. 2005). Findings indicate that research-based strategies used with EO students are also effective with ELLs, although the strategies must be adapted to strengths and needs of ELLs (Calderón et al. 2005).

Diane August and her colleagues (2005) suggest several strategies that appear to be especially valuable for building the vocabularies of ELLs. These strategies include taking advantage of students' first language if the language shares cognates with English, teaching the meaning of basic words, and providing sufficient review and reinforcement. Because English and Spanish share a large number of cognate pairs, the first instructional strategy is especially useful for Spanish-speaking ELLs. These students can draw on their cognate knowledge as a means of figuring out unfamiliar words in English. A second instructional strategy for ELLs is learning the meanings of basic words—words that most EO students already know. Basic words can be found on lists, such as the Dale-Chall List (Chall and Dale 1995). A third instructional strategy that ELLs particularly benefit from is review and reinforcement. These methods include read-alouds, teacher-directed activities, listening to audiotapes, activities to extend word use outside of the classroom, and parent involvement.

CHAPTER

1

Specific Word Instruction

what?
why?
when?
how?

what? **Specific Word Instruction**

> Reading print and understanding words are two conditions needed for success in reading "grade-level" books.
>
> —BIEMILLER, 2005b

Explicit instruction has proven to be an effective way for students to acquire vocabulary knowledge (National Reading Panel 2000). Direct teaching of specific vocabulary words relevant to a given text can deepen students' knowledge of word meanings. The goal is to enable students to "use the instructed words in understanding a text containing those words and to recall the words well enough to use them in speech and writing" (Beck, McKeown, and Kucan 2002). Specific words can be directly introduced through teacher read-alouds or through independently read text.

According to reading researchers (Armbruster, Lehr, and Osborn 2001; Beck et al. 2002; National Reading Panel 2000; Stahl and Fairbanks 1986), specific word instruction should:

- focus on words that are contextualized in literature, important to the text, and useful to know in many situations;

- provide "rich," in-depth knowledge of word meanings—not just repeated definitions;

- provide clear, accessible explanations and examples of word meanings in various contexts, with opportunities for students to discuss, analyze, use, and compare the words in these contexts;

- provide multiple exposures to the words in more than one context;

- engage students in active, deep processing by getting them to use words in new contexts and to create associations among words.

Selecting Words to Teach

Selecting Words to Teach

Though no formula or explicit list yet exists for selecting age-appropriate vocabulary for instruction, in the last few years several researchers have worked out strategies to identify such vocabulary. Isabel Beck and her colleagues (2002) have developed a systematic three-tier method for selecting vocabulary to teach. Margarita Calderón and her colleagues (2005) have modified Beck's tier system for English-language learners. Andrew Biemiller (2005a) and his colleagues are developing a sequenced list of words based on their findings that regardless of grade level, all students acquire words in roughly the same order.

The Three-Tier System

Beck and McKeown (1985) have evolved a system, or algorithm, for selecting the words in a text best suited for direct explanation and focused instruction. In the system, a word is classified according to its level of utility, or tier (Beck et al. 2002). According to these researchers, a mature literate individual's vocabulary basically comprises three tiers of words: Tier-One words consist of basic words, such as *the, and, daddy,* and *food.* Except for English-language learners and students who are word impoverished, these words rarely require instruction in school. Tier-Two words occur frequently in language, are central to comprehension, and are understood by most mature language users. Tier-Two words are the best candidates for explicit instruction. Tier-Three words are low-frequency "specialized" words that are often limited to specific fields, domains of knowledge, or content areas such as social studies or science. Tier Threes should be taught only as they arise.

This concept of word tiers is not an exact science but a helpful guideline for choosing words for instructional attention. The boundaries between the tiers are not always clear cut. Thinking in terms of tiers is just a starting point—a way to frame the task

17

of choosing candidate words for direct vocabulary instruction (Beck et al. 2002). This can be done by a process of elimination: first eliminate the Tier-One words, then the Tier-Three words, and you are likely to arrive at the Tier-Two words.

Guidelines for Using the Three-Tier System

TIER ONE

Ask Yourself . . .
- Is it a basic word whose meaning students are likely to know?
- Is it on the Dale-Chall List (Chall and Dale 1995)?

Examples: between, daddy, food, night, some, walk

Instructional Recommendation These words rarely require instruction, except for English-language learners and students who are word impoverished.

TIER TWO

Ask Yourself . . .
- Is it a word whose meaning students are unlikely to know?
- Is it a word that is generally useful—a "general-purpose word" that students are likely to encounter across a wide variety of domains?
- Can the meaning of the word be explained in everyday language, using words and concepts that are familiar to students?
- What is the word's instructional potential? Is its meaning necessary for comprehension of the text being read?

Examples: balcony, murmur, splendid

Instructional Recommendation These words are candidates for explicit instruction.

TIER THREE

Ask Yourself . . .
- Is it a word whose meaning students are unlikely to know?
- Is it a specialized word that does not appear frequently in written or oral language?
- Is the word specific to a particular content area or subject matter?

Examples: anthracite, mycelium, shoal

Instructional Recommendation These words are explained at point of contact or as the need arises.

Based on Beck et al. 2002; Biemiller 2004.

Categories of Word Knowledge (Average Second-Grade Student)		
Category of Word Knowledge	**Examples**	**Instructional Recommendation**
Words That Are Known Well (known by more than 70 percent of students)	café, drop, fish, flood, kept, listen, loop, match, math, swing, throat	Need no instruction
Words That Are Partially Known (known by 30 to 70 percent of students)	blab, cobra, distant, drama, parcel, possum, react, shimmer, tally, thud, transit	Teach
Word That Are Unlikely to Be Learned (known by less than 30 percent of students)	abrasive, alias, cartilage, character, destitute, franchise, junction, mammoth, polo, sequence, valor	Do not teach; instruction of little value

Based on Biemiller and Slonim 2001.

19

Words are learned in approximately the same order.

—BIEMILLER, 2005a

Sequence of Word Acquisition

According to Andrew Biemiller (2005a), students acquire vocabulary in a relatively well-defined sequence that is ordered by vocabulary size rather than by grade level. For the most part, acquisition of a challenging word is built upon having the knowledge of certain more basic words first (Biemiller and Slonim 2001). For example, a word designated as Tier Two, such as *benevolent* or *leisurely,* may be too advanced in the sequence of word acquisition to be readily learned by a first- or second-grade student (Biemiller 2005b).

Within the sequence of word acquisition, students (regardless of their grade level) know certain word meanings well, partially know others, and are unlikely to learn some (Biemiller 2005a). Biemiller suggests focusing instruction on words that are "partially known" because they tend to be rapidly learned. Above is an example from Biemiller and Slonim's (2001) research, which is still in progress.

20

According to Biemiller (2005a), selecting words to teach in the primary grades must take the sequence of word acquisition into account. Although Biemiller and Slonim (2001) have not yet established a precise word list for each vocabulary level, Biemiller (2004) suggests using an existing word list, the Dale-Chall List (Chall and Dale 1995), to identify words that are "known well," or Tier One, by average first and second graders. For example, to determine whether or not a contextualized word is Tier One or Tier Two, Biemiller recommends checking to see whether or not the word is on the Dale-Chall List. If the word is on the list, it falls into the Tier-One category—a basic word usually not considered a candidate for explicit instruction. However, if you are selecting words for Kindergarten students, students who are word impoverished, or English-language learners, it may be necessary to focus in part on words on the Dale-Chall List (Biemiller 2004).

C O N N E C T

T O   T H E O R Y

From the second paragraph of "Marine Mammals" (p. 204), make a list of all the words that you believe could be good candidates (i.e., Tier Two) for specific word instruction. From the words you select, eliminate any words found on the Dale-Chall List (i.e., Tier One) and any specialized Tier-Three words. From the remaining words, select three target words. Explain your choice of words.

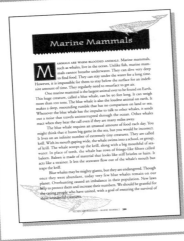

Note: Dale-Chall List words found in second paragraph of "Marine Mammals": *animal, away, blue, call, called, creature, deep, Earth, feet, found, hear, huge, land, largest, long, loudest, many, miles, noise, ocean, one, sea, sends, talk, tons, travels, weigh, whale.*

CONCRETE WORDS

words that can be pictured, felt, or heard, such as *cottage, scalding,* or *shrill*

ABSTRACT WORDS

words that are difficult to demonstrate or picture, such as *cousin, democracy,* or *reluctant*

 **LESSON MODEL**

Introducing Function Words, p. 48

COGNATES

words in two languages that share a similar spelling, pronunciation, and meaning

 **SEE ALSO . . .**

Cognate Awareness, p. 84

Selecting Words for English-Language Learners (ELLs)

In developing a strategy for selecting words for English-language learners (ELLs), Margarita Calderón and her colleagues (2005) borrowed the tier system from Isabel Beck and her colleagues (2002) and then modified it. Using this modified set of criteria for ELLs sometimes results in reclassifying a word's previously designated tier. To guide instruction for ELLs, the modified criteria includes a word's

21

- concreteness (Is the word concrete or abstract? Can it be shown or demonstrated?)

- cognate status (Does the English word have a Spanish cognate?)

- depth of meaning (Does the word have multiple meanings?)

- utility (Is the meaning of the word key to understanding the selection?)

Even though English-only (EO) students are assumed to know most Tier-One words (e.g., words on the Dale-Chall List), this is not always the case for ELLs. For ELLs, these basic words may require explicit instruction. Basic words include both function and content words. Function words, such as *on, under, more, next,* and *some,* alert a reader to the structure of a sentence. Content words, such as *cottage* and *cousin,* carry information or meaning in text. There are two types of content words— words that are concrete and words that are abstract.

Teaching Spanish-speaking students to take advantage of their cognate knowledge can be a powerful tool (August et al. 2005). For ELLs whose first language shares cognates with English, a Tier-Two word that may be challenging for EO students could be considered Tier One for ELLs. Many less frequently used English words are cognates of more frequently used Spanish words; for example, *calabash* and *calabaza.*

Word Tiers and Suggested Teaching Methods for ELLs

Word	EO Student	ELL	ELL Word Classification	ELL Suggested Teaching Method
shoes	Tier One	Tier One	Concrete word: meaning is known, but English label is unknown	Show a picture of the word
ring	Tier One	Tier Two	Concrete word: with multiple meanings	Show a picture of the word; discuss other meanings after reading
share	Tier One	Tier One	Abstract word	Briefly explain word meaning during reading of selection; translate
map	Tier One	Tier One	Cognate: high-frequency English word / high-frequency Spanish word (*map/mapa*)	No explanation; say English word and ask students to provide Spanish word
miles	Tier One	Tier Two	False cognate (the Spanish word *miles* means "thousands")	Point out and give the correct translation
shatter	Tier Two	Tier Two	Concrete word: not a cognate	May not need elaborate discussion
industrious	Tier Two	Tier One	Cognate: low-frequency English word / high-frequency Spanish word (*industrious/industrioso*)	May not need explanation
resist	Tier Two	Tier Two	Abstract word: not a cognate	Explicitly introduce
kayak	Tier Three	Tier Two	Concrete word: not a cognate	Show a picture of the word
calabash	Tier Three	Tier One	Cognate: low-frequency English word / high-frequency Spanish word (*calabash/calabaza*)	May not need explanation
baleen	Tier Three	Tier Two	Specialized word	Define in Spanish if simple English explanation cannot be given

Based on Calderón et al. 2005; Beck et al. 2002.

Rich and Robust Instruction

 **LESSON MODELS**

Children in the primary
grades are generally
"preliterate"—they do
not understand
language in print as
well as they understand
oral language.

— BIEMILLER
& BOOTE, 2006

Rich and Robust Instruction

Effective vocabulary instruction creates rich knowledge of the meaning and uses of words—something that traditional dictionary definition approaches do not provide. This "robust" approach to vocabulary instruction involves not just direct explanation of the meanings of words, but also thought-provoking, playful, and interactive follow-up (Beck et al. 2002). As Beck et al. (2002) put it, robust instruction "offers rich information about words and their uses, provides frequent and varied opportunities for students to think about and use words, and enhances students' language comprehension and production."

23

Using Vocabulary Contextualized in Literature

According to the National Reading Panel (2000), vocabulary instruction should be incorporated into reading instruction, within the context of reading narrative and informational text. Text provides a strong context within which to introduce target words. According to Beck et al. (2002), when words are introduced and explained in the context of a story, students learn word meanings in a situation that is familiar and provides "a rich example of the word's use." Students can learn word meanings from listening to adults read to them or by reading independently on their own.

TEXT TALK: READ-ALOUD METHOD Explicit, teacher-directed vocabulary instruction can complement and enhance traditional storybook reading activities (Coyne et al. 2004). A story can provide a strong context within which to begin the word-meaning explanation. To this goal, Beck and McKeown (2001) developed Text Talk, a project aimed at capturing the benefits of teacher read-alouds. Text Talk has two main goals: (1) to enhance comprehension through interspersed open questions and (2) to enhance vocabulary development. In Text Talk, vocabulary is fully discussed *after* the reading of a story. During reading, the teacher may pause to briefly introduce each of the target words (Beck et al. 2002).

Develop Word Meaning Through…

Student-Friendly Explanations

Teacher-Created Contexts

Active Engagement with Words

METHOD FOR INDEPENDENTLY READ TEXT Generally, the sequence for independently read text differs from the Text Talk read-aloud method in that target words are introduced *before* students read the selection. This helps make unfamiliar words available for students when they encounter them in their reading (Beck et al. 2002). In cases when a word is likely to affect comprehension, the most effective time to introduce its meaning may be at the moment the word is met in text. Introducing the meanings of target words as they are encountered during reading can be done simply and briefly by quickly explaining or defining the word in context.

Introducing Specific Words

Providing word-meaning information is the first step in building word knowledge. To introduce words so that they take root in a student's vocabulary, keep in mind the following: (1) make word meanings explicit through student-friendly explanations, (2) incorporate teacher-created contexts as opposed to text-based contexts, and (3) get students actively engaged in discussing the word meanings right away (Beck et al. 2002).

STUDENT-FRIENDLY EXPLANATIONS Introduce new vocabulary to students by explaining a word's meaning rather than providing a dictionary definition for the word. To develop student-friendly explanations, follow two basic principles: (1) characterize the word and how it is typically used and (2) explain the meaning in everyday language—language that is accessible and meaningful to students (Beck et al. 2002). For example, a dictionary definition for the word *resist* such as "to withstand the force or the effect of" is puzzling rather than helpful. To define *resist* in accessible language, try to frame the concept of resisting in student-friendly terms. Something like

CONNECT TO THEORY

Create a student-friendly explanation for one of the target words you selected from the second paragraph of "Marine Mammals" (p. 204). First look up the dictionary definition. Then develop your explanation using everyday, accessible language and words such as *something, someone,* or *describes.* For additional clarification, fold an example into your explanation. Finally, compare your explanation with the dictionary definition.

> Dictionary definitions are not an effective vehicle for learning word meanings.
>
> **—BECK ET AL., 2002**

"when a person tries not to give in to something" is an example. Now consider whether that captures the full meaning of *resist.* In fact, it omits the idea of *resist* as putting up a struggle. To reflect that idea, we might alter or add to the definition to say "when a person struggles or fights not to give in to something."

TEACHER-CREATED CONTEXTS   Sometimes a word's natural context—in text or literature—is not all that informative or helpful for deriving word meanings (Beck et al. 2002). For this reason, it is useful to intentionally create and develop instructional contexts that provide strong clues to a word's meaning. Instructional contexts are usually created by teachers, but can sometimes be found in commercial reading programs.

ACTIVE ENGAGEMENT WITH WORDS   Provide short, playful, and lively opportunities for students to interact with words and process their meanings right away. This type of active engagement gives students repeated exposures to new words. Some examples of these interactions, using the word *interior,* are shown on the following page.

Active Engagement with Words	Target Word: interior
Questions	Jake thought it would be fun to explore the interior of Alaska. Why might you want to spend time in the interior of your state?
Example or Nonexample	Which one of these two sentences tells about the interior of Oregon? On their vacation, the family visited a lake in central Oregon. On their vacation, the family visited the beaches and coast of Oregon.
Finish the Idea	After a trip to the coast, we headed to the interior of the country because _____ .
Have You Ever . . . ?	Can you describe a place you know about that is located in the interior of your state?
Choices	If what I say could be in the interior of a big island, say "center." If not, don't say anything. • a mountain • an ocean beach • a lighthouse • a small town

In-Depth Word Knowledge

Use the Words

Explore Facets of Word Meaning

Consider Relationships Among Words

Developing In-Depth Word Knowledge

Providing students opportunities to process word meanings at a deeper, more complex level, rich instruction goes beyond definitional information to get students actively engaged in using new words and thinking about word meanings and creating relationships among words (Beck et al. 2002). This breadth and depth of information enables students to establish networks of connections between new words and known words (McKeown and Beck 2004).

Students should practice using a word to ensure that the word becomes an active part of their vocabulary, not just an isolated piece of information. For example, they can talk about situations the word would describe or they can consider instances

when the word would be an appropriate choice. Students can respond to various characteristics of a word, explore the facets of its meaning, and apply the word's meaning in a variety of contexts. One commonly used way to reveal facets of a word's meaning is to have students differentiate between two descriptions of a target word.

Word knowledge is stored in networks of connected ideas, clustered in categories somewhat like a mental filing cabinet. Students should consider relationships among words—how word meanings interact. The more connections that can be built, the more opportunities there are to get at a word's meaning (Beck et al. 2002). Graphic organizers, such as maps, webs, and grids, show how words are related; they visually explore word relationships. They are a concrete way to process, reflect on, and integrate information and make categorical thinking visible. Using graphic organizers is an excellent method of helping students to visualize the abstractions of language. Therefore, they are an effective instructional strategy for English-language learners (Gersten and Baker 2001).

> In a successful vocabulary program, words do not appear as part of a classroom exercise and then drop from sight.
>
> —McKEOWN & BECK, 2004

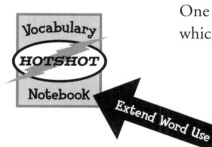

Extending Word Use Beyond the Classroom

Ongoing instruction takes vocabulary learning beyond the classroom. It supports word ownership by students and produces deep and thorough word knowledge that is needed to affect comprehension. The more that students become aware of how words are used and where they are encountered outside class, the greater the chance that they will come to own them (McKeown and Beck 2004). There are many ways to make students conscious of target-word usage beyond the classroom. One of these methods is the Vocabulary Hotshot Notebook, which is described in Chapter 3: Word Consciousness.

why? Specific Word Instruction

> We use words to think;
> the more words
> we know, the finer
> our understanding is
> about the world.
>
> **—STAHL, 1999**

A ccording to the National Reading Panel (2000), explicit instruction in vocabulary can increase vocabulary learning and comprehension. Furthermore, vocabulary instruction should be incorporated into reading instruction. For vocabulary instruction to increase the comprehension of texts that contain unfamiliar words, it must be fairly intensive. This type of instruction provides students with a rich, in-depth knowledge of word meanings. Such in-depth knowledge can help students better understand what they are reading or hearing, and use words accurately. According to William Nagy (2005), "intensive or rich vocabulary instruction requires giving students information about what a word means and about how it is used, and providing them with opportunities to process this information deeply."

Research Findings . . .

Benefits in understanding text by applying letter-sound correspondences to printed material come about only if the target word is in the learner's oral vocabulary.

—NATIONAL READING PANEL, 2000

Preliminary evidence . . . suggests that as late as Grade 5, about 80 percent of words are learned as a result of direct explanation, either as a result of the child's request or instruction, usually by a teacher.

—BIEMILLER, 1999

People with more extensive vocabularies not only know more words but also know more about the words they know.

—CURTIS & GLASER, 1983

The first reason that vocabulary instruction often fails to produce measurable gains in reading comprehension is that much of the instruction does not produce a sufficient depth of word knowledge.

—NAGY, 1988

Suggested Reading . . .

Academic Vocabulary for Middle School Students (2015) by Jennifer Wells Greene & Averil Coxhead. Baltimore, MD: Paul H. Brookes.

Bringing Words to Life: Robust Vocabulary Instruction, 2nd Edition (2013) by Isabel L. Beck, Margaret G. McKeown & Linda Kucan. New York: Guilford.

Foundational Skills to Support Reading for Understanding in Kindergarten Through 3rd Grade (2016) by Barbara Foorman et al. Washington, DC: U.S. Department of Education.

Put Reading First: The Research Building Blocks for Teaching Children to Read, 3rd Edition (2009) by Bonnie Armbruster, Fran Lehr & Jean Osborn. Washington, DC: National Institute for Literacy.

Teaching Academic Content and Literacy to English Learners in Elementary and Middle School (2014) by Scott Baker et al. Washington, DC: U.S. Department of Education.

Teaching and Learning Vocabulary: Bringing Scientific Research to Practice (2005) edited by Elfrieda H. Hiebert & Michael Kamil. London: Routledge.

Vocabulary Instruction: Research to Practice, 2nd Edition (2012) edited by Edward J. Kame'enui & James F. Baumann. New York: Guilford.

when?

Specific Word Instruction

Vocabulary instruction should happen anytime and all the time.

—MCKEOWN & BECK, 2004

When to Teach

It is important to begin direct instruction of specific words as early as possible, in either preschool or Kindergarten. Most of the vocabulary differences among students occur before Grade 3. By Grade 3, students with high vocabularies know thousands more word meanings than children who are experiencing delays in vocabulary development (Biemiller and Slonim 2001). Depending on the instructional situation, specific words can be introduced *before* reading, *during* reading, or *after* reading.

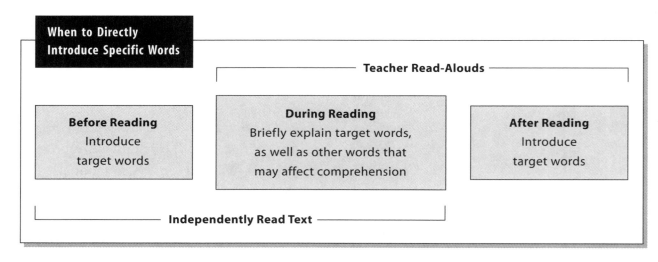

When to Directly Introduce Specific Words

Teacher Read-Alouds

| **Before Reading** Introduce target words | **During Reading** Briefly explain target words, as well as other words that may affect comprehension | **After Reading** Introduce target words |

Independently Read Text

When to Assess and Intervene

The National Reading Panel (2000) suggests that a sound evaluation of a student's vocabulary be based on data from more than a single assessment. The more closely the assessment matches the instructional context, the more appropriate the conclusions about the instruction will be. Assessment that is

How Many Words to Directly Introduce?

Teacher Read-Alouds

KINDERGARTEN About three or four words per book at one or two books per week

GRADE 1 About four or five words per book at one or two books per week

GRADE 2 About five or six words per book at one or two books per week

Independently Read Text

GRADES 2–8 About eight to ten words per selection at one selection per week

Based on Beck et al. 2002.

tied to instruction (e.g., the targeted words) will provide better information about students' specific learning. Standardized tests provide a global measure of vocabulary and may be used to provide a baseline.

Andrew Biemiller (2004) believes that the inability to readily assess vocabulary growth has been a major reason for lack of attention to vocabulary in the primary grades. Standardized vocabulary tests can be used as a baseline. Biemiller thinks teachers can get a general idea of how well students know words by asking them to raise their hand if they know a word and then tell what the word means.

Early, intensive intervention is especially critical for students who enter Kindergarten with impoverished oral vocabularies. Limited vocabulary knowledge places many students at risk for early failure in learning how to read and later failure in comprehending texts. Interventions that increase the effectiveness of storybook reading activities through explicit teaching of word meanings hold promise for decreasing the vocabulary differences among students in the primary grades (Coyne et al. 2004).

Purpose	Vocabulary Assessment	Publisher
Screening	CORE Literacy Library *Assessing Reading: Multiple Measures, 2nd Edition* CORE Vocabulary Screening	Arena Press
Screening Progress Monitoring	Expressive One-Word Picture Vocabulary Test (EOWPVT-4) Receptive One-Word Picture Vocabulary Test (ROWPVT-4)	Academic Therapy Publications
Screening Progress Monitoring	FastBridge AUTOreading ▸ Word Morphology ▸ Matching Synonyms ▸ Vocabulary Words	FastBridge Learning
Screening Progress Monitoring Diagnostic	easy CBM™ ▸ Vocabulary	University of Oregon easycbm.com

how? Specific Word Instruction

LESSON MODEL FOR

Contextualized Vocabulary

Benchmark

• ability to develop in-depth knowledge of word meanings

Grade Level

• Kindergarten–Grade 2

Grouping

• whole class
• small group or pairs

Sample Text

• "Common Sense: An Anansi Tale" (Resources)

Text Talk: Read-Aloud Method

This lesson model is based on Text Talk, a research-based method developed by Isabel Beck and Margaret McKeown and described in *Bringing Words to Life: Robust Vocabulary Instruction* (Beck et al. 2002). In Text Talk, text-specific vocabulary is extensively introduced after a story has been read aloud to students. Using sample text, this lesson model provides an example of how to introduce three previously selected target words. The same model can be adapted and used to enhance vocabulary instruction linked to the read-aloud stories and books in any commercial reading program.

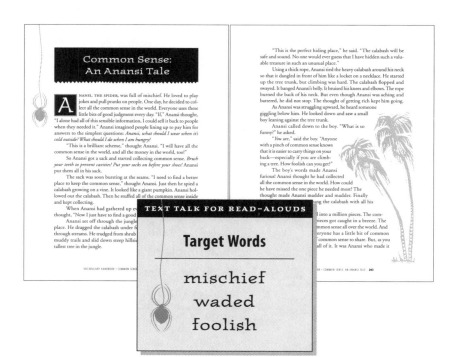

Point out to Spanish-speaking ELLs that *calabash* and *calabaza* are cognates.

Read the Story Aloud

Read aloud the sample text "Common Sense: An Anansi Tale." As you are reading, pause and give a brief explanation for each target word when you come to it, as well as for any words that are likely to affect comprehension. The explanations should not interrupt the flow of the story; target words will be fully explained after reading the story.

- At the target word *mischief,* stop and say: *Mischief means playing tricks on people.*

- At the Tier-Three word *calabash,* stop and say: *A calabash is like a big pumpkin. Have you ever carved a pumpkin on Halloween? You have to hollow out the pumpkin first.*

- At the target word *waded,* stop and say: *Wading is walking through water that is not deep, usually just at your ankles or knees or not higher than your waist.*

- At the target word *foolish,* stop and say: *A foolish person is someone who doesn't have good common sense.*

After Reading the Story

After reading the story, fully introduce the meanings of the target words, one word at a time.

TEXT TALK FOR READ-ALOUDS

Target Word

mischief

Introduce the Target Word

Contextualize the Word   The context of the story provides a familiar situation within which to introduce the word. Say: *The story tells us that Anansi the spider is always up to some mischief.*

Say the Word   Create a phonological representation of the word. Say: *Let's say the word together: mischief.* Ask: *What is the word?* (mischief)

Give a Student-Friendly Explanation   Explain the word's meaning in everyday language—language that is clear and acces-

English/Spanish Cognates

brilliant • brillante

calabash • calabaza

furious • furioso

imagined • imaginó

information • información

jungle • jungla

million • millón

rich • rico

spied • espió

treasure • tesoro

False Cognates

scheme • esquema (diagram)

sensible • sensible (sensitive)

SEE ALSO . . .

Cognate Awareness, p. 84

sible to students. Say: *Mischief is behavior that is a little bit naughty—it's not really bad behavior. Someone who causes mischief likes to tease and play tricks.*

Provide a Different Context   Show how the word can be used in a context different from the story context. Say: *When I found a plastic spider in my bed, I knew someone was up to mischief.*

Engage Actively with the Word   Provide playful opportunities for students to interact with the word and process its meaning right away. Here are some examples:

FINISH THE IDEA   Sentence starters require students to use and apply the meaning of a target word in a different context. Tell students that you are going to start a sentence and you want them to think of an ending. For example, say: *A puppy can get into a lot of mischief. Tell about some mischief a puppy might make. Try to use mischief when you tell about it. You can start out by saying, "My new puppy got into a lot of mischief when _____."*

CHOICES   Making choices enables students to apply the meaning of a target word. Tell students that you are going to name some situations, and if a situation is an example of making mischief, they should say "mischief." If it isn't, they shouldn't say anything. For example, say:

• *Making "rabbit's ears" when someone is taking a picture* ("mischief")
• *Practicing the piano* (no response)
• *Jumping out and scaring someone* ("mischief")
• *Putting salt in the sugar bowl* ("mischief")

Say the Word Again   Reinforce the word's meaning and phonological representation. Ask: *What is the word that describes behavior that is a little bit naughty?* (mischief)

TEXT TALK FOR READ-ALOUDS

Target Word

waded

Introduce the Target Word

Contextualize the Word   The context of the story provides a familiar situation within which to introduce the word. Say: *In the story, Anansi waded through streams.*

Say the Word   Create a phonological representation of the word. Say: *Let's say the word together: waded.* Ask: *What is the word?* (waded)

Give a Student-Friendly Explanation   Explain the word's meaning in everyday language—language that is clear and accessible to students. Say: *Wading has to do with walking through water or mud that is not deep. When you're wading, it is usually not too hard to move your legs to take a step forward.*

Provide a Different Context   Show how the word can be used in a context different from the story context. Say: *Some kids like to wade in puddles after a heavy rain.*

Engage Actively with the Word   Provide playful opportunities for students to interact with the word and process its meaning right away. Here are some examples:

QUESTIONS   Ask questions that require students to apply the target word's meaning. Ask: *If you were hiking and had to cross a stream that had water in it up to your knees, what word would you use to describe how you walked across the stream?* (waded)

CHOICES   Making choices enables students to apply the meaning of a target word. Tell students that you are going to name some places, and if a place is where someone could wade,

36

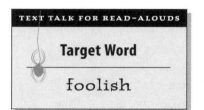

Target Word

foolish

The word *foolish* is found on the Dale-Chall List (Chall and Dale 1995). Biemiller (2005a) considers *foolish* to be a word that is known well by average second graders.

they should say "slish-slosh," the noise someone might make when wading. If it isn't, they shouldn't say anything. For example, say:

- *A supermarket* (no response)
- *A creek* ("slish-slosh")
- *A mud puddle* ("slish-slosh")
- *A hallway* (no response)

Say the Word Again   Reinforce the word's meaning and phonological representation. Ask: *What is the word that describes walking through mud or water that is not deep?* (wading)

Introduce the Target Word

Contextualize the Word   The context of the story provides a familiar situation within which to introduce the word. Say: *In the story, a boy tells Anansi he is very foolish to climb while carrying the calabash in front.*

Say the Word   Create a phonological representation of the word. Say: *Let's say the word together: foolish.* Ask: *What is the word?* (foolish)

Give a Student-Friendly Explanation   Explain the word's meaning in everyday language—language that is clear and accessible to students. Say: *A foolish person is someone who doesn't use good common sense.*

Provide a Different Context   Show how the word can be used in a context different from the story context. Say: *It is foolish to eat ice cream with a toothpick.*

Engage Actively with the Word   Provide playful opportunities for students to interact with the word and process its meaning right away. Here are some examples:

FINISH THE IDEA   Sentence starters require students to use and apply the meaning of a target word in a different context.

Tell students that you are going to start a sentence and you want them to think of an ending. For example, say: *I'd probably feel foolish if I got to school and realized that my shoes didn't match. Think of an example of being foolish. Try to use the word when you tell about it. You can start out by saying, "The most foolish thing I ever did was _____."*

CHOICES Making choices enables students to apply the meaning of a target word. Tell students that you are going to name situations, and if a situation is an example of acting foolish, they should say "tee-hee." If it isn't, they shouldn't say anything. For example, say:

- *Forgetting your jacket on a cold day* ("tee-hee")
- *Brushing your teeth* (no response)
- *Eating a lot of candy before dinner* ("tee-hee")
- *Studying for a spelling test* (no response)

Say the Word Again Reinforce the word's meaning and phonological representation. Ask: *What is the word that describes someone who doesn't have good common sense?* (foolish)

TEXT TALK FOR READ-ALOUDS

Target Words

mischief
waded
foolish

Bring the Target Words Together

After introducing the words one at a time, provide opportunities for students to use all the words together.

ONE QUESTION Using all the target words, develop one thought-provoking question and then challenge students to answer it. For example, ask: *What kind of mischief at the Pie Factory caused the foolish-looking workers to wade through a vat of banana cream?*

QUESTIONS: TWO CHOICES Develop a question in which students must choose the target word that best describes a particular situation. For example, ask: *If you went swimming alone at night, would it be foolish or wading?* (foolish)

QUESTIONS: ONE CONTEXT Using a single context, develop a question for each of the words. Have students answer the

37

Bring the Words Together

38

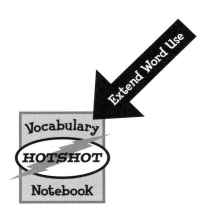

📖 **LESSON MODEL**

Vocabulary Hotshot Notebook, p. 189

set of questions. In this example, the single context is a swimming pool. For example, ask: *What might be foolish to wear in a swimming pool? What mischief could you make if the pool lifeguard wasn't looking? If you had flippers on your feet, could you wade from the low end to the deep end of a swimming pool?*

QUESTIONS: SAME FORMAT Using a uniform format, develop a question for each of the words. Have students explain their answers. For example, ask: *If you are full of mischief, are you being naughty or nice? If you have to wade, would you be in deep water or a puddle? Is being foolish more like acting stupid or acting smart?*

PROMPTS Develop an open-ended discussion prompt for each of the words. Encourage students to respond creatively. For example, ask: *If identical twins wanted to get into some mischief, what could they do? If, after a big storm, your family has to wade to safety, what could have happened? If a friend refused to brush his teeth, what would you say to convince him that he was being foolish?*

Extend Word Use Beyond the Classroom

Developing an in-depth, "rich," and permanent understanding of new vocabulary comes through multiple exposures in more than one context. There are many ways to keep students thinking about and using target words beyond the classroom. One of these methods is the Vocabulary Hotshot Notebook, which is described in Chapter 3: Word Consciousness.

LESSON MODEL FOR

Contextualized Vocabulary

Benchmark

- ability to develop in-depth knowledge of word meanings

Grade Level

- Grade 2 and above

Grouping

- whole class
- small group or pairs

Sample Text

- "Alaska Adventure" (Resources)

Materials

- copies of "Alaska Adventure"

Method for Independently Read Text

This lesson model is based on research-based methods developed by Isabel Beck and her colleagues as described in *Bringing Words to Life: Robust Vocabulary Instruction* (Beck et al. 2002). Using sample text, this lesson model shows how to develop students' knowledge of four previously selected target words. The same model can be adapted and used to enhance vocabulary instruction linked to the text selections in any commercial reading program.

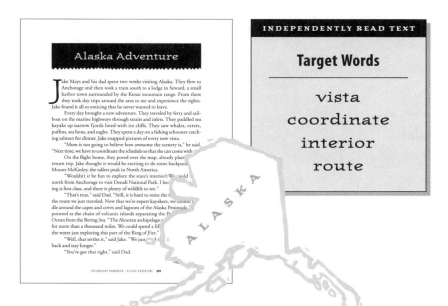

Before Reading the Selection

Before reading the selection, introduce the meanings of the target words, one at a time. Beck et al. (2002) suggest presenting the words "in ways that help them take root in students' vocabularies."

INDEPENDENTLY READ TEXT

Target Word

vista

Point out to Spanish-speaking ELLs that *vista* and *vista* are identically spelled cognates.

   S E E   A L S O . . .

Cognate Awareness, p. 84

Introduce the Target Word

Read and Pronounce the Word   Print the word on the board and have students read and pronounce it. Say: *Let's say the word together: vista.* Ask: *What is the word?* (vista)

Give a Student-Friendly Explanation   Explain the word's meaning in everyday language—language that is clear and accessible to students. Say: *A vista is a faraway scenic view, or a beautiful view from a high place.*

Provide a Different Context   To ensure a clear, explicit concept of the word, develop a sentence with scaffolded questions. In your example, use the target word in a context that is similar to, but different from, the story context. For example, say: *Jake climbed to the top of a hill and took a picture of the beautiful vista that stretched out as far as he could see.* Then ask: *Why did Jake climb the hill? What could he see when he got to the top? So, what do you think vista means?*

Engage Actively with the Word   Provide playful opportunities for students to interact with the word and process its meaning right away. Here are some examples:

QUESTIONS   Ask questions that require students to apply the target word's meaning. Ask: *Where might you go to enjoy a scenic vista?*

FINISH THE IDEA   Sentence starters require students to use and apply the meaning of a target word in a different context. Tell students that you are going to start a sentence and you want them to think of an ending. Say: *The vista stretched out to the horizon from where we stood on the _____.*

HAVE YOU EVER . . . ?   To help students to understand that they have a place for the target word in their vocabularies, have them use the word to describe their own experiences. Ask: *Can you describe the most beautiful vista that you have ever seen? Where were you?*

INDEPENDENTLY READ TEXT

Target Word

coordinate

Point out to Spanish-speaking ELLs that *coordinate* and *coordinar* are cognates.

Introduce the Target Word

Read and Pronounce the Word   Print the word on the board and have students read and pronounce it. Say: *Let's say the word together: coordinate.* Ask: *What is the word?* (coordinate)

Give a Student-Friendly Explanation   Explain the word's meaning in everyday language—language that is clear and accessible to students. Say: *When you coordinate a plan, you match it up with someone else's.*

Provide a Different Context   To ensure a clear, explicit concept of the word, develop a sentence with scaffolded questions. In your example, use the target word in a context that is similar to, but different from, the story context. For example, say: *Mom had to coordinate her work schedule to match Jake's school schedule so that she could get time off to travel to Alaska with him.* Then ask: *What did Mom want to do? What did she have to do to get time off? So, what do you think coordinate means?*

Engage Actively with the Word   Provide playful opportunities for students to interact with the word and process its meaning right away. Here are some examples:

QUESTIONS   Ask questions that require students to apply the target word's meaning. Ask: *How might you coordinate plans to visit a friend?*

FINISH THE IDEA   Sentence starters require students to use and apply the meaning of a target word in a different context. Tell students that you are going to start a sentence and you want them to think of an ending. Say: *My sister and I tried to coordinate our after-school schedules because _____.*

HAVE YOU EVER . . . ?   To help students to understand that they have a place for the target word in their vocabularies, have them use the word to describe their own experiences. Ask: *Can you describe a time when you should have, but did not, coordinate plans with someone? What happened?*

INDEPENDENTLY READ TEXT

Target Word

interior

Point out to Spanish-speaking ELLs that *interior* and *interior* are identically spelled cognates.

Introduce the Target Word

Read and Pronounce the Word   Print the word on the board and have students read and pronounce it. Say: *Let's say the word together: interior.* Ask: *What is the word?* (interior)

Give a Student-Friendly Explanation   Explain the word's meaning in everyday language—language that is clear and accessible to students. Say: *The interior of a state is the central area— the area that is away from the coast, state line, or border.*

Provide a Different Context   To ensure a clear, explicit concept of the word, develop a sentence with scaffolded questions. In your example, use the target word in a context that is similar to, but different from, the story context. For example, say: *Jake wanted to travel inland to explore the interior of the state.* Then ask: *What did Jake want to explore? Where did he have to travel to do it? So, what do you think interior means?*

Engage Actively with the Word   Provide playful opportunities for students to interact with the word and process its meaning right away. Here are some examples:

QUESTIONS   Ask questions that require students to apply the target word's meaning. Ask: *Jake thought it would be fun to explore the interior of Alaska. Why might you want to spend time in the interior of your state?*

FINISH THE IDEA   Sentence starters require students to use and apply the meaning of a target word in a different context. Tell students that you are going to start a sentence and you want them to think of an ending. Say: *After a trip to the coast, we headed to the interior of the country because _____ .*

HAVE YOU EVER . . . ?   To help students to understand that they have a place for the target word in their vocabularies, have them use the word to describe their own experiences. Ask: *Can you describe a place that you know about that is located in the interior of your state?*

INDEPENDENTLY READ TEXT
Target Word
route

Point out to Spanish-speaking ELLs that *route* **and** *ruta* **are cognates.**

Introduce the Target Word

Read and Pronounce the Word   Print the word on the board and have students read and pronounce it. Say: *Let's say the word together: route.* Ask: *What is the word?* (route)

Give a Student-Friendly Explanation   Explain the word's meaning in everyday language—language that is clear and accessible to students. Say: *A route is the way you travel to get from one place to another.*

Provide a Different Context   To ensure a clear, explicit concept of the word, develop a sentence with scaffolded questions. In your example, use the target word in a context that is similar to, but different from, the story context. For example, say: *Dad looked at a map and found the best route to take around the Alaska Peninsula.* Then ask: *What kinds of things are shown on a map? What did Dad use the map for? So, what do you think route means?*

Engage Actively with the Word   Provide playful opportunities for students to interact with the word and process its meaning right away. Here are some examples:

QUESTIONS   Ask questions that require students to apply the target word's meaning. Ask: *Why might you take a different route to school?*

FINISH THE IDEA   Sentence starters require students to use and apply the meaning of a target word in a different context. Tell students that you are going to start a sentence and you want them to think of an ending. Say: *We got lost when Dad took a new route from _____.*

HAVE YOU EVER . . . ?   To help students to understand that they have a place for the target word in their vocabularies, have them use the word to describe their own experiences. Ask: *Can you describe the route that you usually take from home to school?*

43

Read the Selection

Provide copies of the selection "Alaska Adventure." Have students read the text independently, silently or aloud. When text is read aloud in class, stop and give a quick explanation of any target word that is likely to affect comprehension of the selection.

After Reading the Selection

Provide instructional activities that get students actively involved in using and thinking about word meanings.

INDEPENDENTLY READ TEXT

Target Words

vista
coordinate
interior
route

Develop In-Depth Knowledge of the Target Words

DISCUSSION PROMPTS   Use story context as a basis for discussing word meanings with students. For example:

- Jake snapped pictures of every new *vista*. What kinds of things would you see in his photo album?

- What do Mom and Dad have to do to *coordinate* their work schedule and Jake's school schedule?

- What kinds of experiences might Jake have when he visits the *interior* of Alaska?

- Dad wants to retrace the *route* that he and Jake have already taken. Jake wants to see something new. Which route would you take if you had the choice?

Develop In-Depth Knowledge

EXAMPLES OR NONEXAMPLES   Have students differentiate between two descriptions; one is an example of the target word, the other is a nonexample. Here are some models:

- If you think a sentence describes a vista, say "vista."
- ✓ From our campsite, we could see snow-covered mountains. From our campsite, we could see the snack bar.

- If you think a sentence is an example of coordinate, say "coordinate."
- ✓ My team is going to meet at the park at exactly six o'clock. No one told me where or when our team is going to meet.

- If you think a sentence tells about Oregon's interior, say "interior."
- ✓ On their vacation, the family visited a lake in central Oregon. On their vacation, the family visited the coast of Oregon.

- If you think a sentence describes a route, say "route."
- ✓ Turn left where you see the big white house with the red barn. We live next door to the big white house with the red barn.

45

JUXTAPOSITIONS   Challenge students to answer a yes or no question containing two juxtaposed target words. For example:

- Could you *coordinate* plans to meet along a *route*? (yes)

- Could you find a beautiful *vista* in the *interior* of a state? (yes)

CHOICES   Making choices enables students to apply the meaning of a target word. Tell students that you are going to name situations, and if a situation is an example of a vista, they should say "Wow!" If it isn't, they shouldn't say anything. For example:

- *Looking at a faraway view of a mountain peak* ("Wow!")

- *Looking at yourself in the mirror* (no response)

- *Looking at a bug through a magnifying glass* (no response)

- *Looking at the city from the top of a skyscraper* ("Wow!")

English/Spanish Cognates

46

adventure • aventura

archipelago • archipiélago

area • área

coordinate • coordinar

expert • experto

explore • explorar

interior • interior

islands • islas

lagoon • laguna

map • mapa

marine • marino

mountain • montaña

National Park • Parque Nacional

North America • Norteamérica

peninsula • peninsula

route • ruta

salmon • salmón

train • tren

visit • visitar

vista • vista

volcanic • volcánico

False Cognates

come • come (eats)

miles • miles (thousands)

MISSING WORDS As a group, read and discuss cloze sentences and agree on how to complete each one. For example:

- We set up a tripod so that we could photograph the _____ from the top of the hill. (vista)

- It took five phone calls for Mom to _____ the surprise party for Grandpa. (coordinate)

- You can explore the _____ by boat if you travel up the river. (interior)

- Make a map of the _____ we should take to bike from your house to the pool. (route)

TRUE/FALSE Provide 90 seconds for students to respond to true-false statements. For example:

- A vista gives you an up-close view.
  True or false? (false)

- It is hard to make plans unless you coordinate your schedule.
  True or false? (true)

- The interior of the country is close to the beach.
  True or false? (false)

- You can take more than one route to get from place to place.
  True or false? (true)

WORD ASSOCIATIONS After discussing the meanings of the target words, ask students to associate one of the words with a sentence or phrase. For example:

- Which word goes with a scenic view? (vista)

- Which word goes with a plan to meet Mom at the bus stop? (coordinate)

- Which word goes with central Montana? (interior)

- Which word goes with Highway 1 from Mexico to Canada? (route)

Assess Word Knowledge

Assess students' knowledge of the target words by giving them a multiple-choice quiz at the end of the week. Here is an example:

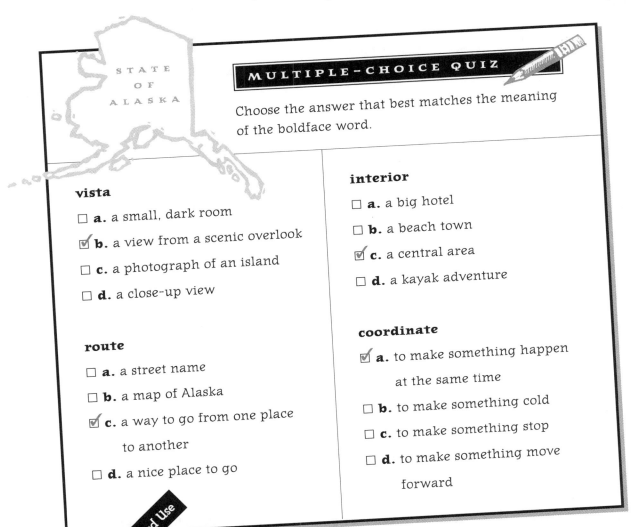

STATE OF ALASKA

MULTIPLE-CHOICE QUIZ

Choose the answer that best matches the meaning of the boldface word.

vista

- ☐ **a.** a small, dark room
- ☑ **b.** a view from a scenic overlook
- ☐ **c.** a photograph of an island
- ☐ **d.** a close-up view

route

- ☐ **a.** a street name
- ☐ **b.** a map of Alaska
- ☑ **c.** a way to go from one place to another
- ☐ **d.** a nice place to go

interior

- ☐ **a.** a big hotel
- ☐ **b.** a beach town
- ☑ **c.** a central area
- ☐ **d.** a kayak adventure

coordinate

- ☑ **a.** to make something happen at the same time
- ☐ **b.** to make something cold
- ☐ **c.** to make something stop
- ☐ **d.** to make something move forward

Extend Word Use

Vocabulary **HOTSHOT** Notebook

📖 **LESSON MODEL**

Vocabulary Hotshot Notebook, p. 189

Extend Word Use Beyond the Classroom

Developing an in-depth, "rich," and permanent understanding of new vocabulary comes through multiple exposures in more than one context. There are many ways to keep students thinking about and using target words beyond the classroom. One of these methods is the Vocabulary Hotshot Notebook, which is described in Chapter 3: Word Consciousness.

LESSON MODEL FOR
Basic Vocabulary

Benchmark

• ability to discriminate the meanings of the prepositions *on* and *under*

Grade Level

• Kindergarten and above, as required

Prerequisite

• mastery of the words *book, desk, chair, pencil, fly, table*

Grouping

• whole class
• small group or pairs

Teaching Chart

• Where Is the Fly? (Resources)

Materials

• props: book, desk, chair, pencil
• PDF of "Where Is the Fly?"

FUNCTION WORDS

Target Word
_____

on

Introducing Function Words

Function words alert a reader or speaker to the structure of the sentence; they are words that have syntactic function. Function words include articles (*a, an, the*), conjunctions (*and, but, or*), helping verbs (*been, should, will*), prepositions (*in, on, over*), and pronouns (*he, she, we*). Most English-only students learn function words in the first stages of language development (Stahl and Nagy 2000). ELLs, however, may be confused about function-word usage and meaning, and can benefit from explicit instruction (Anderson and Roit 1998). This sample lesson model targets the prepositions *on* and *under*. The same model can be adapted and used for introducing other function words.

● ●

Teach/Model

Tell students that they are going to learn a new word that they use often when they speak, read, and write. The word is *on*.

Introduce the Target Word

• Hold up a book. Ask: *What is this?* (a book)
• Point to a desk. Ask: *What is this?* (a desk)
• Put the book on the desk. Emphasizing the word *on*, say: *The book is* on *the desk.*
• Put the book on the floor under the desk. Say: *Is the book on the desk? No.*
• Hold the book under the desk. Say: *Is the book on the desk? No.*
• Put the book on the desk. Say: *Is the book on the desk? Yes, the book is on the desk.*
• Hold the book above the desk. Say: *Is the book on the desk? No.*
• Put the book on the desk. Say: *Is the book on the desk? Yes, the book is on the desk.*

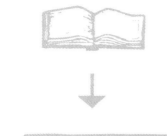

Guided Practice

- Put the book on the desk. Ask: *Is the book on the desk?* (yes)
- Put the book on the floor under the desk. Ask: *Is the book on the desk?* (no)
- Hold the book under the desk. Ask: *Is the book on the desk?* (no)
- Hold the book above the desk. Ask: *Is the book on the desk?* (no)
- Again put the book on the desk. Ask: *Is the book on the desk?* (yes)
- Say: *Say the whole sentence with me. The book is on the desk.*
- Say: *Now repeat the whole sentence by yourselves.* (The book is on the desk.)
- Point to the chair. Ask: *What is this?* (a chair)
- Hold up a pencil. Ask: *What is this?* (a pencil)
- Now put the pencil on the seat of the chair. Ask: *Is the pencil on the chair?* (yes)
- Put the pencil on the floor under the chair. Ask: *Is the pencil on the chair?* (no)
- Hold the pencil under the chair. Ask: *Is the pencil on the chair?* (no)
- Hold the pencil above the chair. Ask: *Is the pencil on the chair?* (no)
- Again put the pencil on the seat of the chair. Ask: *Is the pencil on the chair?* (yes)
- Say: *Say the whole sentence with me. The pencil is on the chair.*
- Say: *Now repeat the whole sentence by yourselves.* (The pencil is on the chair.)

CONTINUED ▷

49

1. SPECIFIC WORD INSTRUCTION   2. WORD-LEARNING STRATEGIES   3. WORD CONSCIOUSNESS

Teach/Model

Tell students that they are going to learn a new word that they use often when they speak, read, and write. The word is *under.*

FUNCTION WORDS

Target Word

under

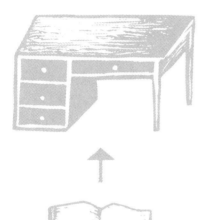

Introduce the Target Word

- Hold up a book. Ask: *What is this?* (a book)
- Point to a desk. Ask: *What is this?* (a desk)
- Put the book on the floor under the desk. Emphasizing the word *under,* say: *The book is* under *the desk.*
- Put the book on the desk. Say: *The book is on the desk.*
- Hold the book under the desk. Say: *The book is under the desk.*
- Put the pencil under the chair. Say: *The pencil is under the chair.*
- Put the pencil on the chair. Say: *The pencil is on the chair.*

Guided Practice

- Put the book under the desk. Ask: *Is the book under the desk?* (yes)
- Put the book on the desk. Ask: *Is the book under the desk?* (no)
- Put the book under the desk. Ask: *Is the book under the desk?* (yes)
- Say: *Say the whole sentence with me. The book is under the desk.*
- Say: *Now repeat the whole sentence by yourselves.* (The book is under the desk.)
- Put the pencil on the chair. Ask: *Is the pencil under the chair?* (no)
- Put the pencil under the chair. Ask: *Is the pencil under the chair?* (yes)
- Say: *Say the whole sentence with me. The pencil is under the chair.*
- Say: *Now repeat the whole sentence by yourselves.* (The pencil is under the chair.)

Guided Mixed Practice

Tell students that now they will practice using the words *on* and *under*.

<table>
<tr><td>

FUNCTION WORDS

Target Words

on

under

</td></tr>
</table>

Practice Using the Target Words—Set 1

- Put the book on the desk. Ask: *Is the book on the desk?* (yes) Say: *Now say the whole sentence.* (The book is on the desk.)
- Put the book under the desk. Ask: *Is the book on the desk?* (no) Ask: *Where is the book?* (The book is under the desk.)
- Again put the book on the desk. Ask: *Where is the book?* (on the desk) Say: *Now say the whole sentence.* (The book is on the desk.)
- Again put the book under the desk. Ask: *Where is the book now?* (under the desk) Say: *Now say the whole sentence.* (The book is under the desk.)
- Put the pencil on the seat of the chair. Ask: *Is the pencil on the chair?* (yes) Say: *Now say the whole sentence.* (The pencil is on the chair.)
- Put the pencil under the chair. Ask: *Is the pencil on the chair?* (no) Ask: *Where is the pencil?* (The pencil is under the chair.)
- Again put the pencil on the seat of the chair. Ask: *Where is the pencil?* (on the chair) Say: *Now say the whole sentence.* (The pencil is on the chair.)
- Again put the pencil under the chair. Ask: *Where is the pencil now?* (under the chair) Say: *Now say the whole sentence.* (The pencil is under the chair.)

CONTINUED ▷

51

FUNCTION WORDS

Target Words

on

under

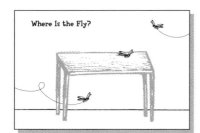

Where Is the Fly?

Practice Using the Target Words—Set 2

Use interactive whiteboard technology to display "Where Is the Fly?"

- Say: *Look at the picture of flies and a table.*
- Point to a fly. Ask: *What is this?* (a fly)
- Point to the table. Ask: *What is this?* (a table)
- Say: *One of the flies is on the table.*
- Point to each fly and ask: *Is this fly on the table?* (Students answer yes or no.)
- Point to the fly that is on the table. Ask: *Where is this fly?* (on the table) Say: *Now say the whole sentence.* (The fly is on the table.)
- Say: *One of the flies is under the table.*
- Point to each fly and ask: *Is this fly under the table?* (Students answer yes or no.)
- Point to the fly that is under the table. Ask: *Where is this fly?* (under the table) Say: *Now say the whole sentence.* (The fly is under the table.)

Independent Practice

Using the models described above, have pairs of students practice identifying whether a book or pencil is on or under a classroom desk, table, or chair. The partners should take turns being "teacher" and "student."

LESSON MODEL FOR

Word Relationships

Benchmarks

- ability to classify grade-appropriate categories of words
- ability to identify and sort common words from within basic categories

Grade Level

- Kindergarten–Grade 1

Grouping

- whole class
- small group or pairs

Text

- "A Lost Button" from *Frog and Toad Are Friends* by Arnold Lobel (New York: Scholastic, 1970)

Materials

- pictures of living and non-living things
- old magazines
- scissors

Concept Picture Sort

Concept picture sorts provide primary students with an opportunity to classify and categorize, adding new information to their existing store of word knowledge. Providing a common frame of reference, read-alouds make great beginnings for concept sorts. This sample lesson model focuses on the differences between living and nonliving things. The same model can be adapted and used to enhance vocabulary instruction in any commercial reading program.

Prep Time

Divide a bulletin board into two sections.

Read the Story

Read aloud to students "A Lost Button" from *Frog and Toad Are Friends.* In the story, Toad loses a button and he and Frog, with the help of a sparrow and a raccoon, retrace their steps to try to find it.

Teach/Model

After reading the story, show a picture of Frog. Say: *Frog is a living thing because he grows and changes.* Post the picture of Frog in the left section of the bulletin board. Show a picture of Toad. Ask: *Is Toad a living thing or not a living thing?* (a living thing) Say: *That's right. Toad is a living thing because he grows and changes. I will post the picture of Toad near the picture of Frog. Frog and Toad are living things; they grow and change.* Show a picture of a button. Say: *A button is not a living thing because it does not grow or change.* Post the picture of the button in the right section of the bulletin board. Show a picture of a chair. Ask: *Is a chair a living thing or not a living thing?* (not

a living thing) Say: *That's right. A chair is not a living thing because it does not grow or change. I will post the picture of the chair near the picture of the button. A button and a chair are not living things; they do not grow or change.*

Guided Practice

Ask: *What are some other living things in the story?* (raccoon, sparrow, cattail, grass, tree) Show pictures of the other living things from the story and have students identify them. Ask: *What are some other not living things in the story?* (table, basket, spool, pincushion, needle) Show pictures of the other not living things from the story and have students identify them. Mix up the pictures. Then, using the following procedure, call on volunteers to add the pictures to the bulletin board in the appropriate category. For example, ask: *Is a table a living thing or not a living thing?* (not a living thing) *How do you know?* (It doesn't

"A Lost Button"

Living Things
cattail
Frog
grass
raccoon
sparrow
Toad
tree

Not Living Things
basket
button
chair
needle
pincushion
spool
table

grow or change.) *Are you going to put the picture of the table under Frog or under the button?* (under the button) Say: *That's right. A table is not a living thing so it goes with the button.* Continue until all pictures have been sorted under the appropriate category.

Independent Practice

Distribute copies of old magazines and ask students to cut out pictures of two living things and two not living things. After students have had time to cut out the four pictures, ask them to put their pictures into two piles. In one pile, they put living things, such as frogs. In the other pile, they put not living things, such as buttons. Then call on volunteers to add their cutouts to the bulletin board. One volunteer at a time, for each picture, ask: *What is your picture? Is it a living thing or not a living thing? Does it belong with Frog or with the button?* When students have identified and matched the category, they add the picture to the bulletin board.

Extend Word Knowledge

Have students sort things within a category. For example, they can sort living things into categories of plants and animals. Explain that the group of living things has both plants and animals. Point out that animals are living things that can move from place to place and plants are living things that can't move.

Say: *I am going to name some living things that are posted on the bulletin board. If I name an animal, say "living animal." If I name a plant, say "living plant." Look at the picture of Frog. Frog can move. Is Frog a plant or an animal?* (animal) *That's right. Frog can jump. Look at the picture of a tree. A tree cannot move. Is a tree a plant or an animal?* (plant) *That's right. A tree stands still.* Continue by discussing the other pictures in the living category. As the categories are identified, move the pictures so that the plants and animals are grouped together.

55

LESSON MODEL FOR

Word Relationships

Benchmarks

- ability to classify words related to a specific concept
- ability to understand and use vocabulary related to specific content

Grade Level

- Grade 2 and above

Grouping

- whole class
- small group or pairs

Sample Text

- "Alaska Adventure" (Resources)

Materials

- Vocabulary Hotshot Notebooks

Point out to Spanish-speaking ELLs that *geography* and *geografía* are cognates.

Semantic Map

Word knowledge exists not as a list of discrete items but as networks of words clustered into categories (Beck et al. 2002). Semantic mapping, an activity for building connections between groups of semantically connected words, is highly flexible and adaptable to a number of different contexts. In semantic mapping, one concept or word is tied graphically to other related words. This sample lesson model focuses on vocabulary related to the study of geography. The same model can be adapted and used to enhance vocabulary instruction in any commercial reading program.

Introduce the Concept

Print the word *Geography* on the board and read it aloud. Tell students that the word *geography* comes from the Greek word *geographia,* which means "earth description." Remind them that geography is the study of the physical features of the earth's surface, such as mountains and rivers.

Brainstorm

Ask students to brainstorm a list of words related to the study of geography. As students brainstorm, list their suggestions on the board. For example, they might suggest terms such as *mountain, ocean, river, island,* or *volcano.* Then add words to the list from the sample text "Alaska Adventure," such as *strait, inlet, fjord, peninsula, peak,* and *archipelago.* If necessary, provide student-friendly explanations, such as the following:

- A *strait* is a narrow strip of water that joins two large bodies of water.
- An *inlet* is a narrow strip of water which goes from the ocean into the land.
- A *fjord* is an inlet with steep cliffs.

- A *peninsula* is a piece of land that sticks out and is almost completely surrounded by water.
- A *peak* is a mountain, or the top of a mountain.
- An *archipelago* is a group of many islands.

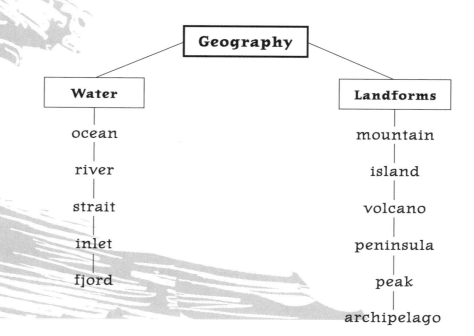

Make the Semantic Map

Tell students that making a semantic map can help them to understand relationships between words. Then have them use the brainstormed list of words to develop a map about geography. Tell students to look at the list of words. Say: *Let's group these words into categories. What do* ocean *and* river *have in common?* (They have to do with water.) Print the word *Water* on the board and draw a line connecting it to the word *Geography.* Next, ask students what other words they could add to this category. (Possible answers: *ocean, river, strait, inlet, fjord*) Add the words to the map. Say: *Can you group the remaining words into a category? What do* island *and* mountain *have in common?* (They are both landforms.) Print the word *Landforms* on the board and draw a line connecting it to the word *Geography.* Next, ask students what other words they could add to this category. (Possible answers: *mountain, island, volcano, peninsula, peak, archipelago*) Add the words to the map.

Read the Selection

After completing the preliminary semantic map, have students read the sample text "Alaska Adventure." Students might read independently, read with a partner, or read the text aloud as a group.

Discuss the Selection and Revise the Map

After reading, ask students if there are any geography terms from the selection that could be added to the map. For example, students might suggest adding *lagoon, cove,* and *cape.* Explain the meaning of each term. Say: *A* lagoon *is a body of shallow water that is separated from the ocean by sand or rock.* Ask: *Where does* lagoon *go on the map?* (under *Water*) Add *lagoon* to the map. Say: *A* cove *is a small bay on the coast.* Ask: *Where does* cove *go on the map?* (under *Water*) Add *cove* to the map. Say: *A* cape *is a piece of land that sticks out into the ocean.* Ask: *Where does* cape *go on the map?* (under *Landforms*) Add *cape* to the map.

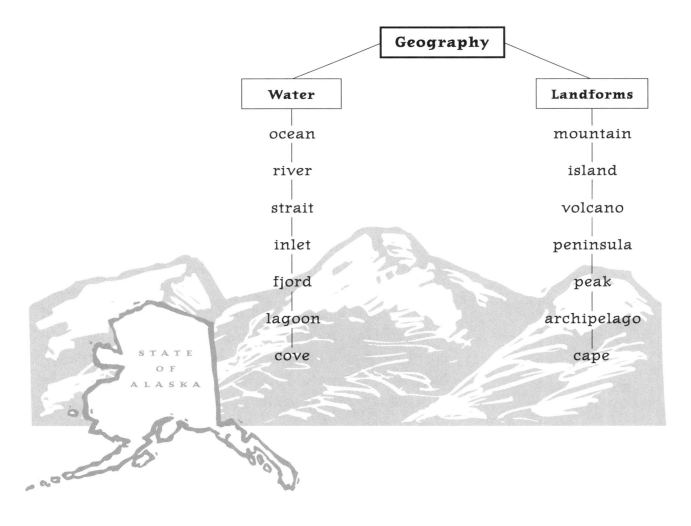

Geography

Water

ocean
river
strait
inlet
fjord
lagoon
cove

Landforms

mountain
island
volcano
peninsula
peak
archipelago
cape

STATE
OF
ALASKA

English/Spanish Cognates

archipelago • archipiélago

fjord • fiordo

island • isla

lagoon • laguna

mountain • montaña

ocean • océano

peak • pico

peninsula • península

strait • estrecho

volcano • volcán

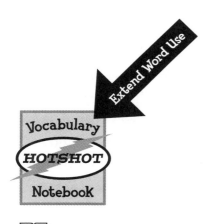

LESSON MODEL

Vocabulary Hotshot Notebook, p. 189

Active Engagement

Engagement and discussion seem to be crucial to the effectiveness of semantic mapping (Stahl and Clark 1987). Provide situations in which students can interact with and discuss the words on the map. Here are some models:

Using the words on the map, have students respond to questions such as the following:

- If you wanted to tie up your boat for the night, would you look for a *strait* or a *cove*?
- If you wanted to go camping, would you pitch your tent in an *inlet* or on an *island*?
- If you wanted to go fishing, would you look for a *lagoon* or a *peninsula*?

Using the words on the map, have students respond to questions such as the following:

- How are a *cape* and a *peninsula* the same? How are they different?
- How are an *inlet* and a *fjord* the same? How are they different?
- Can an *island* have a *cape*? (Yes. A cape is a point of land.)
- Can a *peninsula* have a *lagoon*? (Yes. A peninsula is almost surrounded by water; part of the water could be separated by a ridge of rocks or sand to make a shallow pool.)
- What is the difference between a *peak* and a *volcano*? (A peak is the top of a mountain; a volcano is a peak that erupts.)

Have students use the words in the map to make up their own comparisons.

- Would you rather drive a car on a _____ or a _____ ?
- Would you use a boat to cross a _____ or a _____ ?
- If you wanted to enjoy the view, would you climb a _____ or a _____ ?

LESSON MODEL FOR

Word Relationships

Benchmarks

• ability to categorize words
• ability to compare and contrast features of related words

Grade Level

• Grade 3 and above

Grouping

• whole class
• small group or pairs

Sample Text

• "Alaska Adventure" (Resources)

Materials

• dictionaries
• Vocabulary Hotshot Notebooks

Semantic Feature Analysis

Using a grid rather than a map format, semantic feature analysis is a systematic strategy for exploring and reinforcing vocabulary concepts through use of categorization. Helping students to understand the similarities and differences in related words, this strategy can be used before reading to develop vocabulary before or after reading to reinforce vocabulary (Readence 2004). This sample lesson model focuses on analyzing the category of boats. The same model can be adapted and used to enhance specific word instruction in any commercial reading program.

Select a Category

Select a category to be analyzed. For example, select the category of boats, which is tied to vocabulary in "Alaska Adventure." Tell students that they are going to construct a vocabulary grid that will help them learn the relationships between and among types of boats. On the board, begin a simple grid. Label the grid "Boats."

Add the Category Types

Encourage students to discuss what they know about boats. This may include the boats named in a reading selection such as the sample text "Alaska Adventure," their own boating experiences, or what they have seen on television or in the movies. It may be helpful to show photographs or illustrations of these types of boats. Then, with students' help, print the names of types of boats in the first column of the grid. For example: *ferry, sailboat, kayak, rowboat,* and *cruise ship.*

Add Features

With students' help, decide what features, or characteristics, of boats are to be explored. Start with only a few features and build on them later in the lesson. For this example, features to be examined are whether the boat uses oars, has a motor, has sails, or has an anchor. Across the top row of the grid, print features of boats.

BOATS	oars	motor	sails	anchor
ferry				
sailboat				
kayak				
rowboat				
cruise ship				

Show Feature Possession

Model how the grid can be used to show the features of each type of boat. Say: *If the boat has the feature, I'll write a plus sign. If it does not, I'll write a minus sign. For example, a ferry does not have oars and sails, but it does have a motor and an anchor.* Write a minus sign (–) under oars and sails and a plus sign (+) under motor and anchor. Continue by discussing the features of each boat, marking and discussing the grid as the students respond. Note that feature possession should reflect typical patterns. For example, a small sailboat does not have a motor, but larger sailboats usually do.

BOATS	oars	motor	sails	anchor
ferry	–	+	–	+
sailboat	–	+	+	+
kayak	+	–	–	–
rowboat	+	–	–	+
cruise ship	–	+	–	+

English/Spanish

+ **plus sign • signo más**

− **minus sign • signo menos**

Expand the Grid

Tell students that they are going to help you to expand the grid by adding more types and features. Then guide them in generating names for other types of boats as you add their suggestions to the grid. In our example, students suggest *schooner, tugboat,* and *canoe.* Next guide students in adding some new features, or characteristics, of boats to be analyzed. In our example, students suggest whether a boat has a mast or requires a crew. Help students to complete the grid by analyzing and then marking feature possession of the new types and features.

B O A T S	oars	motor	sails	anchor	mast	crew
ferry	−	+	−	+	−	+
sailboat	−	+	+	+	+	+
kayak	+	−	−	−	−	−
rowboat	+	−	−	+	−	−
cruise ship	−	+	−	+	−	+
schooner	−	+	+	+	+	+
tugboat	−	+	−	+	−	+
canoe	+	−	−	−	−	−

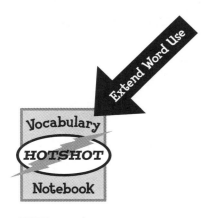

LESSON MODEL

Vocabulary Hotshot Notebook, p. 189

Discuss and Explore the Grid

Discussion seems to be the key to this activity since there are many ambiguities, and discussion of these ambiguities seems to clarify the category, topic, or concept being analyzed (Stahl 1999). Exploring the feature grid is most effective when the students, rather than the teacher, make observations, point out connections, and note similarities and differences. In this final step, have students use the grid to compare and contrast types of boats by examining and discussing how they are related and yet unique. For instance, even though a kayak and a canoe are different, they share similar features. Schooners and sailboats are alike in that they both have masts, but a schooner has at least two masts while a sailboat has one.

63

Further exploration and expansion of the grid may continue, either independently or as a group, particularly as more distinct and discrete features of boats are identified in discussion. Students may also wish to research the category in order to identify specific types of boats, such as skiff or sloop, and explore distinct features, such as rigging and appointments.

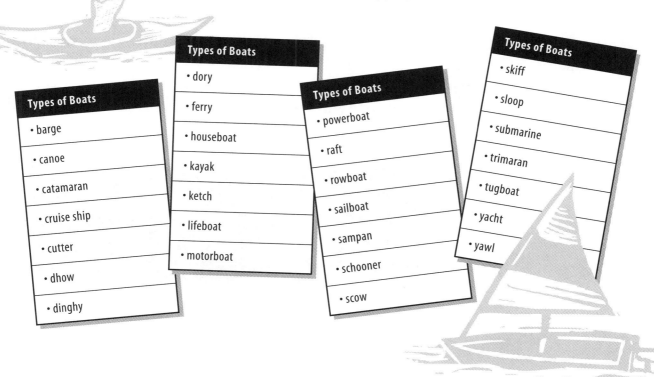

Types of Boats
• barge
• canoe
• catamaran
• cruise ship
• cutter
• dhow
• dinghy

Types of Boats
• dory
• ferry
• houseboat
• kayak
• ketch
• lifeboat
• motorboat

Types of Boats
• powerboat
• raft
• rowboat
• sailboat
• sampan
• schooner
• scow

Types of Boats
• skiff
• sloop
• submarine
• trimaran
• tugboat
• yacht
• yawl

LESSON MODEL FOR
Word Relationships

Benchmark

• ability to acquire in-depth understanding of word meanings

Grade Level

• Grade 3 and above

Grouping

• whole class
• small group or pairs

Sample Text

• "Studying the Sky" (Resources)

POSSIBLE SENTENCES

Target Words

ancient
astronomer
constellation
galaxy
orbit
universe

Possible Sentences

Stahl and Kapinus (1991) found that the use of this prereading strategy significantly improved both students' recall of target word meanings and their comprehension of the selection containing those words. Since students have to use at least two words in each possible sentence, they are required to understand the relationship between the words. Through evaluation of sentence accuracy, students are forced to actively process semantic information about each word (Stahl 1999). This sample lesson model targets specific vocabulary found in "Studying the Sky," a short selection about astronomy. The same model can be adapted and used to enhance specific word instruction in any commercial reading program.

Select the Target Words

Select about six words from the sample text "Studying the Sky" that may be unknown to students, are central to the main idea of the selection, and are adequately defined by context within the selection. Then select about four words from the text that are likely to be known to students.

Introduce the Words

List the following words on the board:

ancient, astronomer, center, constellation, galaxy, orbit, planet, stars, sun, universe

English/Spanish Cognates

ancient • anciano (elderly)

astronomer • astrónomo

constellation • constelación

galaxy • galaxia

orbit • órbita

universe • universo

Tell students that the words on the board will appear in the selection they are about to read, "Studying the Sky." Ask students to share their knowledge of each word. If necessary, provide a brief student-friendly definition of each word.

- *Ancient* describes someone who is very old or something from a very long time ago.
- An *astronomer* is someone who studies planets and stars.
- A *constellation* is a group of stars visible from Earth. The stars create a shape that can be recognized and has a name, such as the Big Dipper.
- A *galaxy* is a group of billions of stars belonging to one star system. Earth is in the Milky Way galaxy.
- An *orbit* is a circular path that a heavenly body or satellite makes around another body in space.
- The *universe* is everything that exists, including all space and matter.

Write Possible Sentences

Next, have students work individually or in pairs to select two or three words from the list on the board. Tell them to make up one sentence that contains at least two of the words and that might appear in the selection they are about to read. Print the suggested sentences on the board and have them read aloud. Include both accurate and inaccurate statements without discussing them. For example, write the following sentences on the board:

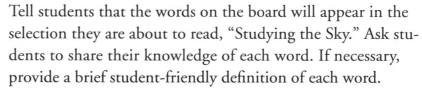

Nine <u>planets</u> <u>orbit</u> around the sun.

A <u>constellation</u> is a great big <u>galaxy</u>.

An <u>astronomer</u> is someone who is <u>ancient</u>.

The <u>sun</u> is the center of the <u>universe</u>.

65

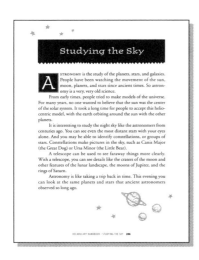

Read the Selection

When students have finished contributing possible sentences using all the target words, have them read, independently or aloud, the selection "Studying the Sky."

Evaluate the Accuracy of the Possible Sentences

After students read the selection, go back and evaluate the accuracy of the possible sentences. Have students look again at the sentences on the board. Encourage them to discuss whether, based on their reading, each sentence is or is not accurate. If they determine that a sentence is accurate, place a checkmark beside it. If a sentence is inaccurate, help students to rewrite the sentence on the board to make an accurate statement. For example:

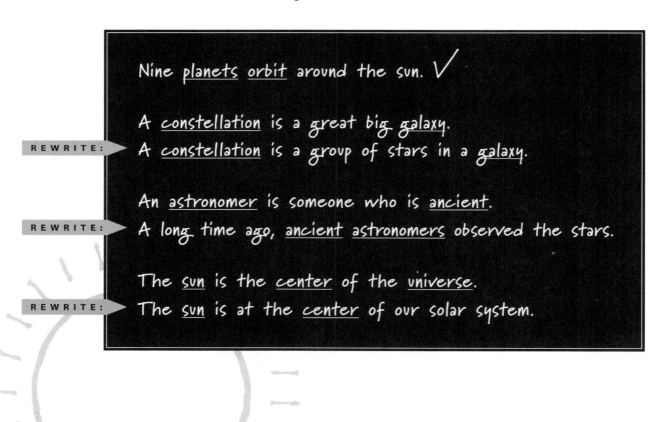

LESSON MODEL FOR

Word Relationships

Benchmark

• ability to acquire in-depth understanding of word meanings

Grade Level

• Grade 2 and above

Prerequisite

• knowing about antonyms and synonyms

Grouping

• whole class
• small group or pairs

Sample Text

• "Alaska Adventure" (Resources)

Activity Master

• Word Map (Resources)

Materials

• copies of Word Map
• Vocabulary Hotshot Notebooks

Word Map

Graphic organizers, such as this word map, help students to visualize how words connect to each other. They help restructure more difficult tasks. When students draw on their prior knowledge to make a concrete, graphic representation of a target word, they show how the word relates to other words and concepts. This sample lesson model targets specific vocabulary found in the sample text "Alaska Adventure." The same model can be adapted and used to enhance vocabulary instruction in any commercial reading program.

67

Teach/Model

Tell students that creating a word map can help them to understand how a new word is related to words and examples they already know. Remind students that in the selection "Alaska Adventure," Jack says, "Mom is not going to believe how awesome the scenery is." In other words, Jack thinks the scenery in Alaska is very impressive. Have students say "What awesome scenery!" in the way Jack would have said it. Tell students that *awesome* is a word that can mean "very impressive" or "very cool."

Then draw from students' experience by asking when they have used the word *awesome*. Ask: *How and when have you used the word* awesome? (Possible responses: *to express excitement, surprise, or joy*) Ask: *What are some examples of how you have used the word* awesome? (Possible responses: *Jack hit an awesome home run. Mom has an awesome new car.*)

On the board, print the target word *awesome* in the center box of a word map, as shown below. Say: *According to Jack, an example of something that is awesome is the scenery in Alaska.* Print *scenery in Alaska* in the example box of the map. Say: *An example of something that is not awesome, or a nonexample, could be a small parking lot.* Print *small parking lot* in the nonexample box of the map. Say: Impressive *is a word that means almost the same as* awesome. Impressive *could be used in place of the word* awesome. Print *impressive* in the synonym box of the map. Say: Ordinary *is a word that means the opposite of* awesome. Print *ordinary* in the antonym box of the map. When the word map is completed, have students discuss it and use the words on it in other contexts.

68   **SYNONYMS**
words that are very close
in meaning

ANTONYMS
words that are opposite or
nearly opposite in meaning

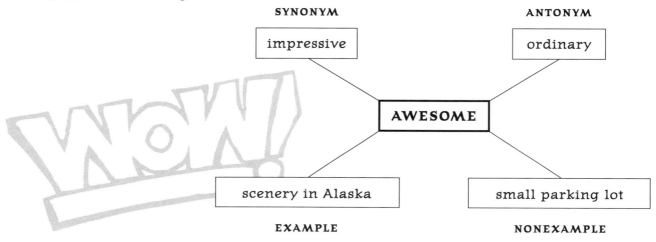

Guided Practice

Using the following activity, explore other examples and non-examples of the word *awesome.* Say: *If the things or situations I describe are examples of something awesome, say "Wow!" If not, don't say anything.*

• a new pair of high-tech running shoes
• cleaning your room
• meeting the president of the United States
• an old pair of slippers
• a colorful rainbow

📖 **SEE ALSO...**

Language Categories, p. 160

Next guide students in making a different word map for *awesome*. Say: *A colorful rainbow could be awesome.* Print *a colorful rainbow* in the example box of the map. Then ask: *What is the opposite of a colorful rainbow?* (Possible response: *a gray day*) Print students' responses in the nonexample box of the map. Continue by having students think of synonyms and antonyms. Say: *The word* impressive *has almost the same meaning as the word* awesome. Ask: *What other words mean almost the same as* awesome? (Possible responses: *amazing, exceptional, cool, extraordinary*) Print students' responses in the synonym box of the map. Say: *The word* ordinary *is one word that means the opposite of* awesome. Ask: *What other words mean the opposite of* awesome? (Possible responses: *dull, unexciting*) Print students' responses in the antonym box of the map. When the word map is completed, have students discuss it and use the words on it in other contexts.

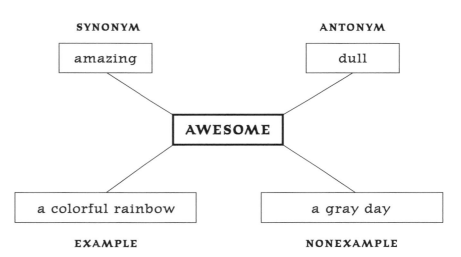

Independent Practice

Extend Word Use

Vocabulary **HOTSHOT** Notebook

📖 **LESSON MODEL**

Vocabulary Hotshot Notebook, p. 189

Have students create their own Word Maps to explore other words they encounter in their reading. For example, students could complete a Word Map for the words *enticing, adventure,* or *interior* from "Alaska Adventure," or they can choose words from other books and stories. Invite volunteers to discuss the target words they have chosen, identify the synonyms and antonyms, and share their examples and nonexamples. Have them write sentences using the words on their maps.

LESSON MODEL FOR
Word-Meaning Recall

Benchmark

- ability to remember word meanings

70

Grade Level

- Grade 3 and above

Grouping

- whole class
- small group or pairs
- individual

Sample Texts

- "Alaska Adventure" (Resources)
- "Studying the Sky" (Resources)

```
KEYWORD METHOD

Target Word
─────────────
archipelago

Keyword
─────────────
pelican
```

Keyword Method

Mnemonic strategies are systematic procedures for enhancing memory. The word *mnemonic* comes from Mnemosyne, the name of Greek goddess of memory. The keyword method, a mnemonic strategy, has been shown to be effective with students who have learning difficulties and those who are at risk for educational failure (Mastropieri and Scruggs 1998). According to the National Reading Panel (2000), the keyword method may lead to significant improvement in students' recall of new vocabulary words. This sample lesson model targets two contextualized vocabulary words. The same model can be adapted and used to enhance recall of vocabulary words in any commercial reading program.

Direct Explanation

Explain to students that you are going to show them how to use the keyword method, a useful strategy for remembering the meanings of vocabulary words. Tell them you are going to model the strategy twice, using the words *archipelago* and *lunar*.

Teach/Model

▶ **1. Define the Target Word**

Read aloud the following sentence from "Alaska Adventure." Then tell students that an *archipelago* is "a group of islands."

> The Aleutian **archipelago** stretches for more than a thousand miles.

Point out to Spanish-speaking ELLs that *archipelago* and *archipiélago* are cognates.

▶ **2. Think of a Keyword for the Target Word**

Say: *To help me remember the meaning of the word* archipelago, *a group of islands, I am going to think of another word, called a "keyword." The keyword is a word that sounds like* archipelago *and also is a word that can be easily pictured. My keyword for* archipelago *is* pelican. Pelican *sounds like* archipelago *and is the name of a water bird with a very large bill.*

▶ **3. Link the Keyword with the Meaning of the Target Word**

Explain to students that the next step is to create an image of the keyword *pelican* and the meaning of the target word *archipelago* interacting in some way. Tell them it is important that the keyword and the meaning actually interact and are not simply presented in the same picture. On the board, sketch a picture of a pelican flying over a group of small islands. Say: *Look at the picture of the pelican flying over the group of islands.* Ask: Pelican *is the keyword for what word?* (archipelago) Say: *Yes,* archipelago. *To recall the meaning of the word* archipelago, *imagine a pelican flying over a group of small islands.*

▶ **4. Recall the Meaning of the Target Word**

Tell students that when they see or hear the word *archipelago*, they should first think of its keyword and then try to remember the picture of the keyword and the meaning interacting. Ask: *What is the keyword for* archipelago? (pelican) *In the sketch, where was the pelican flying?* (over a group of islands) Say: *Right, over a group of islands.* Ask: *So what does* archipelago *mean?* (a group of islands)

KEYWORD METHOD

Target Word

lunar

Keyword

lonely

Point out to Spanish-speaking ELLs that *lunar* and *lunar* are identically spelled cognates.

▶ **1. Define the Target Word**

Read aloud the following sentence from "Studying the Sky." Then tell students that the word *lunar* means "of the moon."

> With a telescope, you can see details like the craters of the moon and other features of the **lunar** landscape, the moons of Jupiter, and the rings of Saturn.

▶ **2. Think of a Keyword for the Target Word**

Say: *To help me remember the meaning of the word* lunar, *"of the moon," I am going to think of a keyword. The keyword is a word that sounds like* lunar *and also is a word that can be easily pictured. My keyword for* lunar *is* lonely. Lonely *sounds like* lunar *and when I think of* lonely *I imagine someone sitting all alone.*

▶ **3. Link the Keyword with the Meaning of the Target Word**

Explain to students that the next step is to create an image of the keyword *lonely* and the meaning of the target word *lunar* interacting in some way. On the board, sketch a picture of a wolf howling at the moon. Say: *Look at the picture of the lonely wolf howling at the moon.* Ask: Lonely *is the keyword for what word?* (lunar) Say: *Yes,* lunar. *To recall the meaning of the word* lunar, *imagine a lonely wolf howling at the moon.*

▶ **4. Recall the Meaning of the Target Word**

Tell students that when they see or hear the word *lunar*, they should first think of its keyword and then try to remember the picture of the keyword and meaning interacting. Ask: *What is the keyword for* lunar? (lonely) *In the picture, what was the lonely wolf doing?* (howling at the moon) Say: *Right, howling at the moon.* Ask: *So what does* lunar *mean?* (of the moon)

2

Word-Learning Strategies

what?
why?
when?
how?

what? Word-Learning Strategies

> If students have the
> task of learning
> tens of thousands of
> words and we can only
> teach them a few
> hundred words a year,
> then they have to do
> a lot of word learning
> on their own.
>
> — GRAVES, 2000

 **LESSON MODELS**

Given the size of vocabularies they need, readers can and must improve their vocabularies independently. Independent word-learning strategies can help students to determine the meanings of unfamiliar words that have *not* been explicitly introduced to them. Knowledge of these types of strategies is generative; it transfers to the learning of new words (Nagy 2005). Directly teaching word-learning strategies, coupled with explicit instruction in specific words, can help students not only to increase their vocabularies, but also to become independent word learners (Baumann et al. 2003). According to the National Reading Panel (2000), effective word-learning strategies include:

- how to use dictionaries to confirm and deepen knowledge of word meanings;

- how to use morphemic (word-part) analysis to derive the meanings of words in text;

- how to use contextual analysis to infer the meanings of words in text.

Dictionary Use

Dictionary use is not as simple as it seems; students frequently have difficulty using the dictionary to define unfamiliar words (Miller and Gildea 1987). Traditionally, instruction in dictionary use has focused on mechanics—how to find an entry alphabetically, how to use guide words, how to separate words into syllables, how to use pronunciation keys—and on having students use information from dictionary definitions to write

Student Dictionaries
Collins COBUILD New Student's Dictionary, 3rd Edition (2005). Glasgow, UK: HarperCollins.
Collins COBUILD School Dictionary of American English (2008). Boston: Heinle.
Heinle's Basic Newbury House Dictionary of American English, 2nd Edition (2004). Boston: Heinle.
Longman Dictionary of American English, 4th Edition (2008). Upper Saddle River, NJ: Pearson.

> Instruction related to dictionary definitions should be simple and direct and involve children in analyzing dictionary definitions in the course of vocabulary instruction.
>
> —STAHL, 2005

sentences. Scott and Nagy (1997) contend that such instruction does not provide students with the guidance they need to make dictionary use an efficient, independent word-learning strategy.

Nonetheless, when used correctly, dictionaries are powerful aids to word understanding. Students can learn greatly from looking up a word and fully processing its definition (Jenkins and Dixon 1983). In fact, McKeown and her colleagues have found that the more students are exposed to definitions, the better they learn words (McKeown, Beck, Omanson, and Pople 1985).

The crucial point is that students should receive instruction in *how to use what they find in a dictionary entry*. They are then better able to translate the "cryptic and conventionalized content" of dictionary definitions into word knowledge they can use (Stahl and Nagy 2000). Teachers should model how to look up the meaning of an unfamiliar word, and how to choose the appropriate definition from an entry to make sure it fits a particular context. Students should be taught to use the dictionary not only when they come across a word they have never seen before, but also to further their knowledge of a word.

Types of Morphemes	
▸ **Free Morphemes** Can Stand Alone as Words	Anglo-Saxon Root Words: *help, play, run*
▸ **Bound Morphemes** Cannot Stand Alone as Words	Prefixes: *dis–, in–, re–, un–*
	Derivational Suffixes: *–ful, –less, –ly*
	Inflectional Suffixes: *–ed, –es, –ing, –s*
	Greek Roots: *bio, graph, scope*
	Latin Roots: *dict, ject, struct*

MORPHEMES

word-part clues; the
meaningful parts of words

 **LESSON MODELS**

Morphemic Analysis

The key instructional elements of morphemic analysis are morphemes, which include root or base words, Greek and Latin roots, and affixes (prefixes and suffixes). Morphemes are also referred to as word-part clues. There are two basic types of morphemes: free and bound. Free morphemes can stand alone as words; they do not have to be combined with other morphemes to make words. Anglo-Saxon root words are examples of free morphemes. Bound morphemes cannot stand alone; they must be attached to, or "bound" to, other morphemes to make words. Affixes (prefixes and suffixes) and Greek and Latin roots are examples of bound morphemes. By learning about morphemes, and the ways in which they contribute to the meaning of a word, students can build a foundation for independent word learning. Morphemic analysis can be an especially effective word-learning strategy for use with content-area text.

Explicit instruction in word-part clues (morphemes) typically involves teaching students the meanings of word parts, how to disassemble words into word parts, and how to reassemble the word parts to derive word meaning (Edwards et al. 2004;

Baumann et al. 2005). According to Biemiller (2005a), the meaning of unfamiliar affixed words can be derived when encountered if the meaning of the root words and affixes are known.

Root Words and Word Families

A root or base word is a single word that cannot be broken into smaller words or word parts. Root words are words from which many other words are formed. Knowing the meaning of one root word can provide a bridge to the meaning of other words related in meaning, or words belonging to a word family. Nagy and Anderson (1984) propose teaching word families, which include a root word and its derived forms. Their analysis of printed school English made clear that a large number of words that students encounter in reading are derivatives or inflections of familiar root words.

Compound Words

An Anglo-Saxon compound word contains two free morphemes, or word parts. The meaning of some compound words is the same as the sum of its two parts; for example, *doghouse* and *bluebird.* Other compound words have a meaning that differs from the meaning of the sum of its two parts; for example, *butterfly* and *airline.*

ROOT WORD

a single word that cannot be broken into smaller words or parts

WORD FAMILY

a group of words related in meaning

 **LESSON MODELS**

Word Families, p. 112

Compound Words, p. 109

77

Using Word-Part Clues to Derive Word Meaning		
Step	**Action**	**Example Word: disagreement**
1	Look for the Root Word. *What does it mean?*	agree = to have the same opinion
2	Look for a Prefix. *What does it mean?*	dis = not or opposite
3	Look for a Suffix. *What does it mean?*	ment = state or quality of something
4	Put the Meanings of the Word Parts Together. *What is the meaning of the whole word?*	dis + agree + ment = state or quality of not having the same opinion

Based on Baumann et al. 2003, 2005.

Facts About Prefixes

Twenty prefixes account for 97 percent of the prefixed words in school reading materials

Four prefixes (*un–*, *re–*, *in–*, and *dis–*) account for 58 percent of all prefixed words

PREFIX

a word part added to the beginning of a root word that changes its meaning

SUFFIX

a word part added to the end of a root word that changes its meaning

 **LESSON MODELS**

Word-Part Clues: Prefixes, p. 115

Word-Part Clues: Suffixes, p. 121

Prefixes

Affixes that come before root words are called prefixes. A prefix can alter the meaning of the root word to which it is "fixed," or attached. Graves (2004) gives several reasons why prefixes are particularly worth teaching and are well suited for instruction: (1) there is a relatively small number of prefixes, (2) prefixes are used in a large number of words, (3) prefixes tend to be consistently spelled, (4) prefixes are easy to identify because they occur at the beginning of words, and (5) prefixes usually have a clear lexical meaning.

Graves (2004) recommends that teachers provide explicit instruction in the most frequently used prefixes. White, Sowell, and Yanagihara (1989) suggest teaching prefixes in the order of their frequency, varying that order according to the demands of students' instructional texts. These researchers found that twenty prefixes account for about 97 percent of the prefixed words in printed school English. Four prefixes (*un–, re–, in–,* and *dis–*) account for about 58 percent of prefixed words.

Suffixes

Affixes that follow root words are called suffixes. A suffix can alter the meaning or function of the root word to which it is "fixed," or attached. There are two kinds of suffixes: inflectional and derivational. Inflectional suffixes (e.g., *–s, –es, –ed, –ing*) change the form of a word but not its speech part; these include verb forms, plurals, and comparatives and superlatives. Derivational suffixes (e.g., *–ful, –less*) are like prefixes in that they alter a root word's meaning. Inflectional suffixes are the most frequently occurring suffixes in school reading materials, while derivational suffixes appear in less than a quarter of all the words that contain suffixes (White et al. 1989). Even though derivational suffixes appear less frequently, researchers recommend that teachers do spend time directly teaching them (Edwards et al. 2004; Stahl 1999).

SEE ALSO . . .

Most Frequent Prefixes, p. 80

Most Frequent Suffixes, p. 81

LIMITATIONS Morphemic analysis, though useful, does not always work. By only considering word-part clues, students may be misled about the true meaning of a word. White, Sowell, and Yanagihara (1989) pointed out some pitfalls: (1) some prefixes are not consistent in meaning (e.g., *in–* means both "not" and "in"), (2) sometimes the removal of what appears to be a prefix leaves no meaningful root word (e.g., *uncle*), and (3) sometimes the removal of what appears to be a prefix or a suffix leaves a word that is not obviously related in meaning to the whole word (e.g., *increase, bashful*).

CONNECT TO THEORY

Morphemic analysis does not always work. Using a student anthology or content-area textbook, look for words beginning with the letters *un, re, in,* or *dis.* From the group of words, select one example for each of the following four categories: (1) does not have a prefix and root word, (2) has a prefix and root word, (3) combined meanings of prefix and root word result in the meaning of the whole word, and (4) combined meanings of prefix and root word do not result in the meaning of the whole word. For an example, refer to the chart on page 120.

WORD-PART CLUE EVALUATION

WORD	Does Not Have Prefix and Root Word	Has Prefix and Root Word	Prefix + Root Word = Meaning	Prefix + Root Word ≠ Meaning

Most Frequent Prefixes Attached to Free Morphemes			
Prefix	**Meaning**	**Example**	**Percent**
un–	not	unkind	26%
re–	again, back	redo, return	14%
in–, im–, il–, ir–	not	injustice, impossible	11%
dis–	not, opposite of	disagree	7%
en–, em–	cause to	encode, empower	4%
non–	not	nonsense	4%
in–, im–	in, on	insane, imprint	4%
over–	too much	overdo	3%
mis–	wrong	misfire	3%
sub–	under	sublease	3%
pre–	before	preview	3%
inter–	between	interact	3%
fore–	before	foreclose	3%
de–	not, opposite	deactivate	2%
trans–	across	transplant	2%
super–	above	superstar	1%
semi–	half	semicircle	1%
anti–	against	antiwar	1%
mid–	middle	midway	1%
under–	below	undersea	1%
All others			3%

Based on White, T. G., J. Sowell, and A. Yanagihara 1989.

Most Frequent Suffixes Attached to Free Morphemes

Suffix	Meaning	Example	Percent
–s, –es	more than one	books, boxes	31%
–ed	past-tense verbs	played	20%
–ing	verb form/present participle	running	14%
–ly	characteristic of	quickly	7%
–er, –or	one who	worker, actor	4%
–ion, –tion, –ation, –ition	act, process	collection, infusion	4%
–able, –ible	can be done	comfortable	2%
–al, –ial	having characteristics of	personal	1%
–y	characterized by	jumpy	1%
–ness	state of, condition of	kindness	1%
–ity, –ty	state of	formality	1%
–ment	action or process	enjoyment	1%
–ic	having characteristics of	linguistic	1%
–ous, –eous, –ious	possessing the qualities of	joyous	1%
–en	made of	wooden	1%
–er	comparative	higher	1%
–ive, –ative, –itive	adjective form of a noun	active	1%
–ful	full of	careful	1%
–less	without	fearless	1%
–est	comparative	longest	1%
All others			7%

Based on White, T. G., J. Sowell, and A. Yanagihara 1989.

81

Common Greek and Latin Roots in English

Root	Meaning	Origin	Example
astro	star	Greek	astronaut
aud	hear	Latin	audible
dict	say, tell	Latin	dictate
geo	earth	Greek	geology
graph	write, record	Greek	autograph
meter	measure	Greek	barometer
mit, miss	send	Latin	submit, mission
ology	study of	Greek	morphology
ped	foot	Latin	pedal
phon	sound	Greek	phonograph
port	carry	Latin	transport
spect	see	Latin	inspect
struct	build, form	Latin	construct
tele	from afar	Greek	telephone

 **LESSON MODELS**

Word-Part Clues: Roots, p. 125

Latin and Greek Number Words, p. 172

Greek and Latin Roots

Greek and Latin roots are bound morphemes that cannot stand alone as words in English. Most Greek roots appear in combination with each other. For this reason, they are often called combining forms. Most Latin roots appear in combination with one or more affixes. Words of Greek and Latin origin are especially prevalent in English. About 60 percent of the words in English text are of Greek and Latin origin (Henry 1997). A relatively small number of Greek and Latin roots appear in hundreds of thousands of words (Henry 2003).

Latin-origin words used in science and technical fields account for a large number of English/Spanish cognates.

From the middle grades on, words with Greek and Latin roots form a large proportion of the new vocabulary that students encounter, primarily in their content-area textbooks. In English, Greek-based words tend to be related to math and science. Bear et al. (1996) suggest introducing Greek roots before Latin roots because their meaning is more apparent, or less abstract, than Latin roots. Stahl and Nagy (2000) believe that a distinction should be made between instructional time spent on Greek roots used in specialized scientific language and time spent on Latin roots whose meanings are more general-purpose.

Research on teaching roots is sparse; researchers and educators are divided as to whether it is profitable to teach them (Stahl and Nagy 2000). Researchers argue that a Latin root's meaning is not always strongly related to the meaning of a word containing the root. For example, knowing that Latin root *port* means "carry" may help with *portable* or *transport,* but probably does not help someone derive the meaning of *portico* or *portly.*

83

Select a Greek and Latin root from the chart on page 82. Beginning with the example word, brainstorm a list of at least five words that have the same root and also are related in meaning. Here are some examples:

- Greek root *astro* meaning "star": *astronaut, asterisk, asteroid, astrology, astronomy*

- Latin root *spect* meaning "see": *inspect, inspector, inspection, prospector, spectator*

84

COGNATES

words in two languages that share a similar spelling, pronunciation, and meaning

FALSE COGNATES

pairs of words that are spelled the same or nearly the same in two languages but do not share the same meaning

Cognate Awareness

One method of building vocabulary among English-language learners whose language shares cognates with English is to capitalize on students' first-language knowledge (August et al. 2005). Cognates are words in two languages that share a similar spelling, pronunciation, and meaning. Students often can draw on their knowledge of words in their native language to figure out the meanings of cognates in English. Because of their common Latin and Greek roots, as well as the close connections between English and the Romance languages, English and Spanish share a large number of cognate pairs.

Second-language learners do not automatically recognize and make use of cognates (Nagy et al. 1993; Nagy 1988). Recent studies indicate that explicitly identifying cognates supports English-language acquisition for Spanish-speaking students (Carlo et al. 2004; Bravo, Hiebert, and Pearson 2005). When selecting cognates for instruction, it is important to focus on cognates that Spanish speakers are likely to know from their everyday Spanish use (Bravo, Hiebert, and Pearson 2005). These types of cognates include pairs that are high-frequency words in both English and Spanish (e.g., *animal/animal*) and pairs that have a high-frequency Spanish word and a low-frequency English word (e.g., *enfermo/infirm*). Dressler (2000) found that it is possible for Spanish-speaking students to make connections between cognates on the basis of sound alone. Thus, students who are not literate in Spanish but are orally proficient in the language can benefit from instruction in cognate awareness, as can students who are literate in Spanish.

English/Spanish cognates fall into several different categories: cognates that are spelled identically, cognates that are spelled nearly the same, cognates that are pronounced nearly the same, and false cognates. False cognates are pairs of words that are spelled identically or nearly the same in two languages but do not share the same meaning.

Categories of Cognates in English and Spanish

Category	Definition	English	Spanish
▸ **Cognates** have the same meaning	spelled identically	chocolate* doctor hotel	chocolate doctor hotel
	spelled nearly the same	class family music	clase familia música
	pronounced nearly the same	baby equal peace	bebé igual paz
▸ **False Cognates** have different meanings	spelled identically	pan pie red	pan (bread) pie (foot) red (net)
	spelled nearly the same	exit rope soap	éxito (success) ropa (clothing) sopa (soup)

*Based on Rodriguez 2001. *English word borrowed from Spanish*

85

CONNECT TO THEORY

You may be surprised how many English/Spanish cognates can be found in a typical text selection. Using the list below, identify cognates in the sample text "Marine Mammals" (p. 204); for example, *animals* and *animales*. Then consult an English/Spanish dictionary to make sure the meaning of the Spanish cognate has the same meaning as the English word in the text. (See Answer Key, p. 198.)

SPANISH WORDS: animales, marino, océano, imposible, aire, criatura, comparación, impulso, reaccionar, miles, número, grupo, filtros, material, gigantes, abundante, planeta, población, proteger

86

Students who are more skilled at reading and more knowledgeable about word meanings are those most able to learn word meanings from context.

—SCOTT, 2005

 **LESSON MODELS**

Context Clues, p. 129

Introducing Types of Context Clues, p. 133

Applying Types of Context Clues, p. 139

CONTEXT CLUES
words or phrases that give readers hints or suggestions to the meaning of unfamiliar words

Contextual Analysis

Contextual analysis involves inferring the meaning of a word by scrutinizing surrounding text. Instruction in contextual analysis usually involves teaching students to identify and employ both generic and specific types of context clues. Research on the important role context plays in incidental word learning is compelling (Nagy and Scott 2000; Swanborn and de Glopper 1999). However, there is less information about whether teachers can enhance this "natural effect" through explicit instruction on how to employ context clues (Baumann et al. 2002). Kuhn and Stahl (1998) noted that the lack of research evidence about effective contextual analysis instruction is "disappointing." But since students encounter such an enormous number of words as they read, some researchers believe that even a small improvement in contextual analysis ability has the potential to produce substantial, long-term vocabulary growth (Nagy et al. 1985, 1987; Swanborn and de Glopper 1999).

Types of Helpful Context Clues

Several studies suggest that simple practice in inferring word meanings from context may be just as effective as instruction in specific context-clue types (Kuhn and Stahl 1998). However, according to an analysis by Fukkink and de Glopper (1998), "clue instruction appears to be more effective than other instruction types or just practice." Baumann and his colleagues (2002, 2003, 2005) recommend instruction in five types of helpful context clues: definition, synonym, antonym, example, and general.

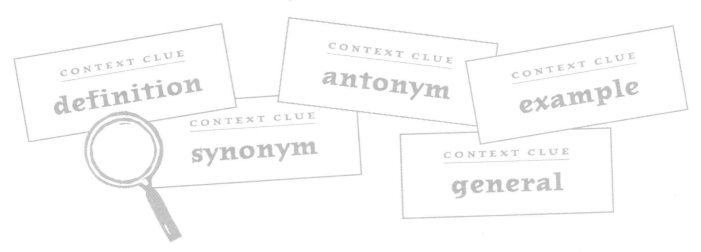

TYPES OF HELPFUL CONTEXT CLUES

Type	Description	Example Sentence
Definition	The author provides a direct definition of an unfamiliar word, right in the sentence. • SIGNAL WORDS: *is, are, means, refers to*	A <u>conga</u> *is* a barrel-shaped drum.
Appositive Definition	A type of definition clue. An appositive is a word or phrase that defines or explains an unfamiliar word that comes before it. • SIGNAL WORD: *or* • SIGNAL PUNCTUATION: set off by commas	At night you can *see* <u>constellations</u>, *or* groups of stars, in the sky.
Synonym	The author uses another word or phrase that is similar in meaning, or can be compared, to an unfamiliar word. • SIGNAL WORDS: *also, as, identical, like, likewise, resembling, same, similarly, too*	My dog Buck travels everywhere with me. My friend's <u>canine</u> buddy travels everywhere with him, *too*.
Antonym	The author uses another word or phrase that means about the opposite of, or is in contrast with, an unfamiliar word. • SIGNAL WORDS: *but, however, in contrast, instead of, on the other hand, though, unlike*	I thought the movie would be weird, *but* it turned out to be totally <u>mundane</u>.
Example	The author provides several words or ideas that are examples of an unfamiliar word. • SIGNAL WORDS: *for example, for instance, including, like, such as*	In science we are studying <u>marine mammals</u> *such as* whales, dolphins, and porpoises.
General	The author provides some nonspecific clues to the meaning of an unfamiliar word, often spread over several sentences.	Einstein rode his bike everywhere. He thought driving a car was way too <u>complicated</u>.

Based on Baumann et al. 2003, 2005.

87

Unhelpful Context Clues

One of the problems in teaching contextual analysis is that it does not always work; sometimes the context does not provide enough clues to determine a word's meaning (Edwards et al. 2004). Many naturally occurring written contexts found in literature and expository texts are not all that informative for inferring word meanings; they are not equally rich and are sometimes unreliable (Beck et al. 2002). It is important to inform students that there are limits to contextual analysis. Beck and her colleagues (2002) describe two types of unhelpful context clues: misdirective and nondirective. They explain that unhelpful contexts are not in themselves wrong or a misuse of language. The context surrounding an unfamiliar word may communicate the author's ideas well, but provide no help in inferring the meaning of the word.

UNHELPFUL CONTEXT CLUES

Type	Description	Example Sentence
Misdirective	These clues seem to direct the reader to an incorrect meaning for the word.	"She looks so happy and beautiful in her party dress," said Jim <u>maliciously</u>.
Nondirective	These clues seem to be of no assistance in directing the reader toward any particular meaning for the word; the unfamiliar word could have a number of inferable meanings.	When I answered the phone, I heard my sister's <u>agitated</u> voice.

Based on Baumann et al. 2002.

CONNECT TO THEORY

Context clues can be either helpful or unhelpful. Using a student anthology or content-area textbook, look for words that may be unfamiliar to students. From target-word context, find one example of each type of context clue. For each context sentence or sentences, identify the target word by underlining it in blue; the signal words and signal punctuation by underlining them in red; and the context clues by underlining them in green.

CONTEXT CLUES

Type of Context Clue	Target Word	Context Sentence or Sentences
• **Definition**		
• **Appositive Definition**		
• **Synonym**		
• **Antonym**		
• **Example**		
• **General**		
• **Misdirective**		
• **Nondirective**		

When morphemic and contextual analysis instruction is provided in combination, the effects appear to be just as powerful as when it is provided in isolation.

—**BAUMANN ET AL., 2002**

 **LESSON MODELS**

Introducing The Vocabulary Strategy, p. 143

Practicing The Vocabulary Strategy, p. 150

Combined Morphemic and Contextual Analysis

In recent studies, James Baumann and his colleagues (2003, 2005) explored the effectiveness of teaching middle-grade students (Grades 4–8) to use morphemic and contextual analysis in tandem. The studies' primary instructional strategy was called the Vocabulary Rule, an integrated approach that combines the use of context clues and word-part clues. The researchers concluded that students can be taught to use word-part and context clues to learn vocabulary independently and that combined instruction is just as effective as separate instruction (Baumann et al. 2005).

89

The Vocabulary Strategy chart below is based upon Baumann's combined approach. The five steps take students through a complete process that integrates three previously learned strategies: using context clues to infer a word's meaning, using word-part clues to derive a word's meaning, and using the dictionary to confirm a word's meaning.

THE VOCABULARY STRATEGY

To figure out the meaning of an unfamiliar word that you come across while reading:

1. **Look for Context Clues** in the Words, Phrases, and Sentences Surrounding the Unfamiliar Word

2. **Look for Word-Part Clues** Within the Unfamiliar Word
   A. Try to Break the Word into Parts. (If you can't, skip to Step 3.)
   B. Look at the Root Word. What does it mean?
   C. Look at the Prefix. What does it mean?
   D. Look at the Suffix. What does it mean?
   E. Put the Meanings of the Word Parts Together. What is the meaning of the whole word?

3. **Guess the Word's Meaning** (Use Steps 1 and 2.)

4. **Try Out Your Meaning in the Original Sentence** to Check Whether or Not It Makes Sense in Context

5. **Use the Dictionary**, if Necessary, to Confirm Your Meaning

Based on Baumann et al. 2003, 2005.

Word-Learning Strategies

Students learn
words independently
when they are
taught strategies
for determining the
meanings of
words by analyzing
morphemic
and contextual clues.

—EDWARDS ET AL., 2004

There are many more words to be learned than can be directly taught in even the most ambitious program of vocabulary instruction. Even when instruction in specific words is as robust as possible, students still need to learn much of their vocabulary independently (Graves et al. 2004). A great deal of research now supports direct instruction in word-learning strategies as one of the components of a comprehensive vocabulary program (National Reading Panel 2000). While the research has not yet proven the efficacy of these word-learning strategies in all cases or over long periods, it has shown that such strategies are generally effective in that they help students determine the meaning of many unfamiliar words encountered in their reading (Baumann et al. 2002, 2003).

Two widely used methods of helping students learn to deal with unfamiliar words on their own are contextual and morphemic analysis. According to Nagy (1988), "there is no doubt that skilled word learners use context and their knowledge of prefixes, roots, and suffixes to deal effectively with new words." Therefore, readers who are skillful in applying morphemic and contextual analysis have the potential to independently acquire the meanings of many unfamiliar words.

Research Findings . . .

Instruction in morphemic and contextual analysis provides an important complement to a vocabulary program that includes instruction in specific words as well as independent reading and word play and word consciousness activities.

—BAUMANN ET AL., 2003

More than 60% of the new words that readers encounter have relatively transparent morphological structure—that is, they can be broken down into [meaningful] parts.

—NAGY ET AL., 1989

For every word a child learns, we estimate that there are an average of one to three additional related words that should also be understandable to the child, the exact number depending on how well the child is able to utilize context and morphology to induce meaning.

—NAGY & ANDERSON, 1984

Teaching people to learn better from context can be a highly effective way of enhancing vocabulary development.

—STERNBERG, 1987

Suggested Reading ...

Teaching Academic Content and Literacy to English Learners in Elementary and Middle School (2014) by Scott Baker et al. Washington, DC: U.S. Department of Education.

Teaching and Learning Vocabulary: Bringing Scientific Research to Practice (2005) edited by Elfrieda H. Hiebert & Michael Kamil. London: Routledge.

Teaching Vocabulary in All Classrooms, 5th Edition (2015) by Camille Blachowicz & Peter J. Fisher. New York: Pearson.

Teaching Word Meanings (2006) by Steven A. Stahl & William E. Nagy. London: Routledge.

The Vocabulary Book: Learning & Instruction, 2nd Edition (2016) by Michael F. Graves. New York: Teacher's College Press.

Vocabulary Instruction: Research to Practice, 2nd Edition (2012) edited by Edward J. Kame'enui & James F. Baumann. New York: Guilford.

Word-Learning Strategies

Teaching word-learning strategies will take a lot of time during initial instruction.

—GRAVES, 2000

When to Teach

Effective word-learning strategy instruction should provide students with sufficient opportunities to "internalize the strategies and receive the support required to apply them across multiple contexts over time" (Baumann et al. 2005). On the other hand, it is important not to dedicate inordinate amounts of time to such lessons. Graves (2000) suggests that middle-grade students spend two to four hours a week in *initial* word-learning strategy instruction—about three weeks out of the year. The average amount of instructional time for the whole school year would be about 20 minutes per week.

Based on word frequency data, some researchers recommend that instruction in morphemic analysis may be appropriate for students from about fourth grade on (Nagy, Diakidoy, and Anderson 1993; White, Power, and White 1989). However, as early as second grade, teachers may begin instruction in compound words, word families, and simple prefixes and suffixes.

New vocabulary can be acquired through the skillful use of context clues in reading and listening. Beginning in Kindergarten, when reading aloud, the teacher can model the use of context clues to determine the meaning of unfamiliar words or concepts. In Grades 2 and 3, students learn how to use context clues in independently read text. In Grades 4 and above, students learn about the types of context clues and their uses.

Sequence of Instruction

Contextual Analysis

Context clues in read-alouds

Context clues in independently read text

Types of context clues: definition, synonym, antonym, example, general

Morphemic Analysis

Compound words

Prefixes and derivational suffixes with Anglo-Saxon root words

Greek roots

Latin roots

Greek and Latin roots plus affixes

When to Assess and Intervene

The National Reading Panel (2000) suggests that a sound evaluation is based on data from more than a single vocabulary assessment. The more closely the assessment matches the instructional context, the more appropriate the conclusions about the instruction will be. Assessment that is tied to instruction will provide better information about students' specific learning.

According to Blachowicz and Fisher (2002), what is central to the assessment of word-learning strategies is a process, such as thinking aloud or self-evaluation, that reveals the students' metacognitive thinking. For example, teachers can ask students to "Say out loud the thinking you were doing as you figured out the meanings of the words" (Baumann et al. 2002). Simple alternative, authentic assessment formats also can be useful, and the multiple-choice format of most standardized tests also provides a global measure of vocabulary and may be used as a baseline.

93

Purpose	Norm-Referenced Vocabulary Assessment	Publisher
Diagnostic	Gates-MacGinitie Reading Tests, 4th Edition (GMRT)	Houghton Mifflin Harcourt
Diagnostic	Peabody Picture Vocabulary Test, 4th Edition (PPVT-4)	Pearson
Diagnostic	Stanford Diagnostic Reading Test, 4th Edition (SDRT-4)	Pearson
Diagnostic	Woodcock Reading Mastery Tests, 3rd Edition (WRMT™-III)	Pearson

how?

Word-Learning Strategies

LESSON MODEL FOR

Dictionary Use

Benchmark

• ability to effectively use the dictionary to define words in context

Grade Level

• Grade 2 and above

Prerequisite

• knowing how to locate words in a dictionary

Grouping

• whole class
• small group or pairs

Sample Texts

• "Weekend Campout" (Resources)
• "Percussion Instruments" (Resources)

Materials

• dictionaries
• PDF of "Weekend Campout"
• PDF of "Percussion Instruments"
• Vocabulary Hotshot Notebooks

Using the Dictionary

Since students frequently have difficulty using the dictionary to find definitions of unknown words, they need to be taught how to work effectively with a tool that they will use throughout their school years and that many adults use almost daily (Graves et al. 2004; Miller and Gildea 1987). This sample lesson model can be adapted and used to enhance dictionary-use instruction in any commercial reading program.

Direct Explanation

Tell students that they are going to be learning how to use a dictionary to define, clarify, and confirm the meaning of unfamiliar words. Explain that it is worthwhile to learn how to find the correct definition in the dictionary and that using the dictionary isn't always as simple as it may seem.

Say: *You don't just use a dictionary to look up a word you've never seen or heard of before. Often you look up a word that you think you already know but whose actual meaning you want to discover. Sometimes you know what a word means but you want to get a more exact definition. Sometimes you are not exactly sure what a word means and you want to confirm that you are using it correctly. Wondering about words is a good start when it comes to using a dictionary. Anytime you use a word and think, "Does that word mean what I think it means?" you can reach for a dictionary and find out.*

Guidelines for Using the Dictionary

 The first entry that you find for a word might not be the one you are looking for. Make sure you have found and read all the entries for a word.

 When you find the right entry, read all the different meanings, or definitions, that the dictionary gives for the word. Do not just read part of the entry.

 Choose the dictionary meaning that best matches the context in which the word is used. One meaning will make sense, or fit better, than any other.

Display Guidelines for Using the Dictionary, such as the example shown above. Discuss the guidelines aloud, explaining each one of the points. Make sure that students understand the kinds of information they can derive from a dictionary definition.

Teach/Model

Display a transparency of "Weekend Campout." Underline the word *pitch* in the fourth sentence. Tell students that you are going to show them how to use a dictionary to determine the meaning of the word *pitch*. Explain that they might have a feel for what the word *pitch* means without being exactly sure. Then read aloud the following sentence:

Weekend Campout

THE FRANCO FAMILY loves to be outdoors. They spend almost every weekend camping. Fay Franco adores camping more than anything. She will even pitch her tent in the backyard just to sleep outside.

Fay has been to lots of campgrounds. Mar Vista Shores is her favorite. The campsites are in the tall trees. Each spot has a beach view.

At Mar Vista Shores, noisy birdcalls wake Fay early. She hears loud squawking and jumps up for breakfast. Then she packs a picnic. Fay and her dad drive to the trailhead. It is the place where the hiking trails start. They choose a path to take. Dad carries a daypack. It holds a first aid kit, sweatshirts, food, and water. The path leads sharply uphill to a waterfall. It is a steep climb! They hungrily devour their lunch by the riverbank. From the rocks, Fay can watch the water plummet over the cliff.

In the afternoon, Fay and her mom go to the seashore. Mom is a rock hound. She hunts for neat-looking stones. Fay makes sandcastles. Using wet sand, she builds high walls and towers. Sometimes she pokes around the tide pools. She looks for crabs and starfish in the rocks along the beach.

At dinnertime, the Franco family usually has a sunset cookout. They light a campfire. They roast hotdogs. The sky turns pink over the water. Nighttime falls. Fay gets into her sleeping bag. She looks up to see the stars twinkle overhead.

Fay thinks that weekend campouts are almost perfect. The only flaw comes when it is time to go home.

VOCABULARY HANDBOOK • WEEKEND CAMPOUT **287**

DICTIONARY USE

Target Word

pitch

> **She will even <u>pitch</u> her tent in the backyard just to sleep outside.**

Have students look up the word *pitch* in the dictionary; a possible dictionary entry appears below.

> **¹pitch** /pich/ *vb* **1 :** to throw a baseball to a batter **2 :** to set up and fix firmly in the ground **3 :** to fall or plunge forward with force
> **²pitch** *n* **1 :** a throw or toss **2 :** amount of slope **3 :** highness or lowness of a sound
> **³pitch** *n* **1 :** a dark, sticky substance that is made from tar **2 :** resin from pine trees

Read All the Entries

Refer to the first guideline. Ask students how many dictionary entries there are for the word *pitch*. (In the example given here, there are three.) Have students read all the entries and choose the one that seems to fit the meaning they are looking for. (In the example given here, it is the first entry.)

Read All the Different Meanings in an Entry

Refer to the second guideline. Ask students how many different meanings, or definitions, they find in the first entry. (Answers will vary depending on what dictionary is used. In the example given here, there are three meanings in the first entry.) Then invite a volunteer to read all three meanings in the first entry. Remind students not to stop when they come to the meaning they think they are looking for but to read the whole entry all the way through.

Choose the Meaning that Makes Sense

Now refer to the third guideline. Tell students to choose a definition for *pitch* from the first entry that they think makes sense in the context of the original sentence. For example, say: *In the sentence, I don't think that* pitch *has anything to do with throwing a baseball. I don't think she would throw a baseball at the tent in the backyard.* Continue with the other choices, talking through the reasoning that goes into eliminating the definitions that will not work. Then guide students to conclude that the meaning "to set up and fix firmly in the ground" is the correct meaning for *pitch*. Now have them try out the dictionary meaning they selected in the original sentence to confirm whether or not it makes sense. Say: *In the sentence, I am going to substitute* set up *for the word* pitch *to see if it makes sense. "She will even set up her tent in the backyard just to sleep outside." Yes, that makes sense.*

Guided Practice

Use interactive whiteboard technology to display "Percussion Instruments." Underline the word *pitch* in the fourth paragraph. Then read aloud the following sentence:

> **A drum's <u>pitch</u> depends on the size and tightness of the drumhead.**

Tell students that in this sentence the word *pitch* is used in a different context than it was used in "Weekend Campout." Then guide students to use the same dictionary entries to determine the meaning of the word *pitch* in this sentence. Remind students to refer to the Guidelines for Using the Dictionary. When students have analyzed all of the possible entries and definitions, discuss which meaning best fits. Then have students substitute the dictionary meaning they selected in the original sentence. For example, in this sentence "a drum's throw" doesn't make sense, but "a drum's highness or lowness of sound" does make sense.

97

Percussion Instruments

From primitive cave dwellers to modern city dwellers, people have always played percussion instruments. A percussion instrument is any musical instrument that you play by striking or hitting using either sticks or your hands. There are many kinds of percussion instruments, including drums, cymbals, and xylophones.

Of all the percussion instruments, drums are the most prevalent. They are commonly found all over the world. Every culture has developed its own type of drum. The drums may differ from culture to culture, place to place, and group to group, but all of them possess the same basic elements. They usually have a hollow shell, or frame, and a round drumhead.

The shell can come in many shapes and sizes. Shells are usually made out of metal or wood. They can be shallow like a snare drum's or deep like a conga drum's. They can be shaped like a cereal bowl, an hourglass, or even a kettle. The shell acts like a speaker to amplify the sound, or make it louder. A small drum, like a bongo, will sound faint compared to the huge noise made by a big bass drum used in a marching band.

The drumhead is usually made from an animal hide. The animal hide, or skin, is stretched tight over the drum shell. When the drummer hits the drumhead, it vibrates, or moves very quickly back and forth. This vibration creates a resonant, or deep and rich, sound. A drum's pitch depends on the size and the tightness of the drumhead. A smaller, tighter drumhead makes a higher-pitched sound.

Drumbeats are like beating hearts. You can hear their rhythms through the ages.

VOCABULARY HANDBOOK • PERCUSSION INSTRUMENTS **285**

DICTIONARY USE

Target Word

pitch

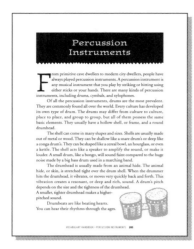

98

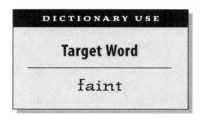

LESSON MODEL

Vocabulary Hotshot Notebook, p. 189

Independent Practice

Continue to display "Percussion Instruments." Point to and underline the word *faint.* Then read aloud the following sentence:

> **A small drum, like a bongo, will sound <u>faint</u> compared to the huge noise made by a big bass drum used in a marching band.**

Have students refer to the Guidelines for Using the Dictionary as they find the appropriate dictionary definition for *faint.* (Possible response: *something that is not strong*) Remind students to choose the meaning that makes sense in the context of the sentence and to confirm their choice by substituting the dictionary definition they selected in the original sentence. After students have looked up the word and determined its meaning, encourage volunteers to model the process.

Encourage students to use the dictionary on a regular basis so that they become comfortable with it and with the procedure for finding word meanings. Invite students to share information they come across when they are learning about unfamiliar words or when they are verifying meanings for words that are familiar but not precisely known.

LESSON MODEL FOR
Dictionary Use

Benchmarks

- ability to choose the appropriate dictionary definition
- ability to use the dictionary to verify a word's meaning

Grade Level

- Grade 3 and above

Grouping

- whole class
- small group or pairs

Prerequisite

- Using the Dictionary

Sample Text

- "Alaska Adventure" (Resources)

Activity Master

- PAVE Map (Resources)

Materials

- PDF and copies of PAVE Map
- dictionaries
- Vocabulary Hotshot Notebooks

PAVE Procedure

Developed by Bannon et al. (1990), PAVE stands for the components of this strategy: prediction, association, verification, and evaluation. In the PAVE Procedure, students predict a word's meaning using sentence context, verify its meaning by consulting the dictionary, evaluate the word's predicted meaning, and associate the word's meaning to an image (Blachowicz and Fisher 2002). This sample lesson model targets specific vocabulary found in the sample text "Alaska Adventure." The same model can be adapted and used to enhance vocabulary instruction in any commercial reading program.

99

Direct Explanation

Tell students that they are going to learn how to complete a PAVE Map. To complete the PAVE Map, they will use sentence context and a dictionary to confirm a target word's predicted definition. Explain that knowing how to follow the PAVE Procedure may help them to determine the appropriate meaning of an unfamiliar word.

Teach/Model

Read aloud the sample text "Alaska Adventure." Then use interactive whiteboard technology to display the PAVE Map. Tell students that you are going to take them through a step-by-step procedure for completing a PAVE Map for the word *vista*. Then model the procedure described on the following pages.

PAVE MAP

1 Context Sentence:
Jake snapped pictures of every new vista.

2 Target Word: vista

3 Predicted Meaning: nice view

7 Word Image

4 Sentence Using Word's Predicted Meaning:
From our motel room, we can see a vista of the parking lot.

5 Word's Dictionary Definition: a distant view from a high place

6 Revised Sentence Using Verified Definition:
From the scenic overlook, there is a spectacular vista of snow-covered mountains that goes on as far as the eye can see.

PAVE PROCEDURE

Target Word

vista

English-Language Learner

Point out to Spanish-speaking students that *vista* and *vista* are identically spelled cognates.

▶ 1. Copy the Context Sentence

On the map, point to and read aloud Step 1, Context Sentence. Say: *I'm going to find and copy the context sentence in which the word* vista *appears.* On the PAVE Map, print the sentence "Jake snapped pictures of every new vista." and read it aloud. Say: *In "Alaska Adventure," this is the context sentence in which the word* vista *appears.*

▶ 2. Print the Target Word

On the map, point to and read aloud Step 2, Target Word. Say: *Next, I'm going to print the target word* vista *on the map.* On the map, print the word *vista.* Then say: *Let's say the word together:* vista.

▶ 3. Predict the Word's Meaning

On the map, point to and read aloud Step 3, Predicted Meaning. Tell students that next you are going to use sentence context

P A V E

Prediction

Association

Verification

Evaluation

to predict the meaning of the word *vista*. Say: *I predict that* vista *means "nice view" because in the sentence, Jack is taking pictures. People like to take pictures of nice views.* Print the predicted meaning on the map.

> ▶ **4. Write a Sentence Using the Word's Predicted Meaning**

101

On the map, point to and read aloud Step 4, Sentence Using Word's Predicted Meaning. Say: *Now I'll make up a sentence using my predicted meaning of the word* vista—*"nice view." Here is my sentence: "From our motel room, we can see a vista of the parking lot."* Print the sentence on the map.

> ▶ **5. Use the Dictionary to Verify the Word's Meaning**

On the map, point to and read aloud Step 5, Word's Dictionary Definition. Say: *Now, I am going to use a dictionary to verify my predicted meaning of the word* vista. *I've got to be sure to choose a definition that makes sense in the context of the sentence in which the word is used. First, I am going to check all definitions and find the one that is closest in meaning.* Read aloud the following sample dictionary entry:

---

vista 1. A beautiful, distant view from a high place. **2.** A mental picture of a series of events in the past or future.

Say: *It looks like the first definition of* vista, *"a beautiful, distant view from a high place," is the one I should use. In my predicted definition, I thought* vista *meant "nice view." But to be more precise, a vista is more than a nice view. It is a distant view from a high place. I think a scenic overlook or the top of a mountain would be a good place to see a vista. I am going to write the dictionary definition for* vista *on the map.* On the map, write the definition, "a beautiful, distant view from a high place."

CONTINUED ▷

PAVE PROCEDURE

Target Word

vista

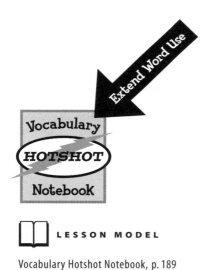

LESSON MODEL

Vocabulary Hotshot Notebook, p. 189

▶ **6. Revise the Sentence Using the Word's Verified Definition**

On the map, point to and read aloud Step 6, Revised Sentence Using Verified Definition. Tell students that now you will revise your original sentence. Say: *Now I'm going to revise my original sentence so it has the sense of looking out from a high place to a view in the distance. Can you picture me at a scenic overlook looking out over hundreds of miles to a range of snow-capped mountains?* On the map, write a revised sentence using the dictionary definition. For example, "From the scenic overlook, there is a spectacular vista of snow-covered mountains that goes on as far as the eye can see."

▶ **7. Draw a Picture to Associate the Word's Meaning**

On the map, point to and read aloud Step 7, Word Image. Tell students that drawing a picture, or image, of a word may help them to remember its meaning. On the map, make a quick sketch of a snow-covered mountain peak as seen from a distance. Say: *This image will help me to remember that a vista has to do with a distant view from a high place.*

Guided Practice

Give students each a copy of the PAVE Map. Choosing a possibly unfamiliar target word from a reading or content-area textbook, guide students through the steps of the PAVE Procedure as described above. This time, as you model filling in the PAVE Map transparency, have students follow along by copying what you write onto their copies of the map. Encourage students to complete Steps 6 and 7 on their own, developing revised sentences and sketching their own word images.

PAVE MAP

1 Context Sentence:

They had come to a stream which twisted and tumbled between high rocky banks, and Christopher Robin saw at once how dangerous it was. "It's just the place," he explained, "for an <u>Ambush</u>." "What sort of bush?" whispered Pooh to Piglet.

2 Target Word: ambush

3 Predicted Meaning: an accident

7
"Boo!"

Word Image

4 Sentence Using Word's Predicted Meaning:

Your bike ambush was not my fault.

5 Word's Dictionary Definition: a surprise attack made from a hiding place

6 Revised Sentence Using Verified Definition:

They hid in the thick grass until it was time for the ambush.

PAVE PROCEDURE

Target Word

ambush

Independent Practice

Give students each another copy of the PAVE Map. Ask them to choose an unfamiliar word from a selection or book they are reading and complete a PAVE Map for the word.

An example of a completed PAVE Map for the target word *ambush* in an excerpt from *Winnie the Pooh* by A. A. Milne is shown above. You may wish to ask volunteers to present their word to the rest of the class. Here is an example of a student presentation: *The target word was* ambush. *It was in this sentence: "It's just the place," he explained, "for an Ambush." I predicted that* ambush *meant "accident." From the dictionary, I found out that it means "a surprise attack made from a hiding place." So, the original sentence meant that this was just the place for a surprise attack. The sentence I wrote was: "They hid in the thick grass until it was time for the ambush." To remember the meaning of the word, I drew a picture of a bush saying, "Boo!"*

LESSON MODEL FOR
Dictionary Use

Benchmarks

• ability to complete a Concept of Definition Map
• ability to recognize and write a good dictionary definition

Grade Level

• Grade 3 and above

Grouping

• whole class
• small group

Sample Texts

• "Percussion Instruments" (Resources)
• "Marine Mammals" (Resources)

Activity Master

• Concept of Definition Map (Resources)

Materials

• copies of "Percussion Instruments"
• PDF and copies of Concept of Definition Map
• copies of "Marine Mammals"
• dictionaries and other references
• Vocabulary Hotshot Notebooks

104

Concept of Definition Map

According to Schwartz and Raphael (1985), a Concept of Definition Map can help students to develop a clear, concrete idea of what "knowing" a word really means. A Concept of Definition Map includes the three elements of a good definition: (1) the overarching category to which the word belongs: What is it? (2) the important features or characteristics of the word or concept: What is it like? and (3) specific examples: What are some examples? This sample lesson model works best with nouns. The same model can be adapted and used to enhance vocabulary instruction in any commercial reading program.

Direct Explanation

Tell students that knowing the parts of a good definition will help them to analyze whether or not they "really know" the full meaning of a word or concept. Explain that completing a Concept of Definition Map will help them to understand the three elements of a good definition: the general category to which the word belongs, the defining features or characteristics of the word, and some examples of the word.

Teach/Model

Give students copies of the sample text "Percussion Instruments" and then read aloud the selection. Use interactive whiteboard technology to display the Concept of Definition Map. Print the word *drum* in the center box of the map. Tell students that using information about drums from the selection will help them learn about the parts of a dictionary definition.

Complete the Map

WHAT IS IT? Point to the heading What Is It? and ask a volunteer to read it aloud. Say: *A definition usually identifies the general category to which the word belongs. According to the text,*

CONCEPT OF DEFINITION MAP

What Is It?

percussion instrument

What Is It Like?

a hollow shell

DRUM

a drumhead

played by striking
with sticks or hands

bass   conga   bongo   snare

What Are Some Examples?

Percussion Instruments

From primitive cave dwellers to modern city dwellers, people have always played percussion instruments. A percussion instrument is any musical instrument that you play by striking or hitting using either sticks or your hands. There are many kinds of percussion instruments, including drums, cymbals, and xylophones.

Of all the percussion instruments, drums are the most prevalent. They are commonly found all over the world. Every culture has developed its own type of drum. The drums may differ from culture to culture, place to place, and group to group, but all of them possess the same basic elements. They usually have a hollow shell, or frame, and a round drumhead.

The shell can come in many shapes and sizes. Shells are usually made out of metal or wood. They can be shallow like a snare drum's or deep like a conga drum's. They can be shaped like a cereal bowl, an hourglass, or even a kettle. The shell acts like a speaker to amplify the sound, or make it louder. A small drum, like a bongo, will sound faint compared to the huge noise made by a big bass drum used in a marching band.

The drumhead is usually made from an animal hide. The animal hide, or skin, is stretched tight over the drum shell. When the drummer hits the drumhead, it vibrates, or moves very quickly back and forth. This vibration creates a resonant, or deep and rich, sound. A drum's pitch depends on the size and the tightness of the drumhead. A smaller, tighter drumhead makes a higher-pitched sound.

Drumbeats are like beating hearts. You can hear their rhythms through the ages.

VOCABULARY HANDBOOK · PERCUSSION INSTRUMENTS **285**

a drum is a percussion instrument. I am going to print percussion instrument *in the box under What Is It?* Print the words *percussion instrument in the box.*

WHAT IS IT LIKE?   Point to the heading What Is It Like? and ask a volunteer to read it aloud. Say: *A good definition usually includes important defining features or characteristics that show how the word is different from other members of its category. According to the selection, the features or characteristics of a drum include a hollow shell and a drumhead, played by striking with sticks or hands. I am going to print these features in the boxes below the heading What Is It Like?* Print the three features in boxes below the heading.

WHAT ARE SOME EXAMPLES?   Point to the heading What Are Some Examples? and ask a volunteer to read it aloud. Say: *A definition sometimes gives examples of the word. The selection* *names the following kinds or types of drums: snare, conga, bongo, and bass. I am going to print the names of these drums in the boxes above the heading What Are Some Examples?* Print the names of the drums in boxes above the heading.

Use the Map to Write a Definition

Parts of a Dictionary Definition
category
What Is It?
features
What Is It Like?
examples
What Are Some Examples?

Point out that a dictionary definition often follows the same structure as the parts of the map. A dictionary definition specifies the category to which a word belongs (What Is It?), its important features or characteristics (What Is It Like?), and some examples or types (What Are Some Examples?).

Display the following incomplete sentences and read them aloud by saying: *A drum is a blank. It has blank, blank, and blank. Some types of drums are blank, blank, and blank.*

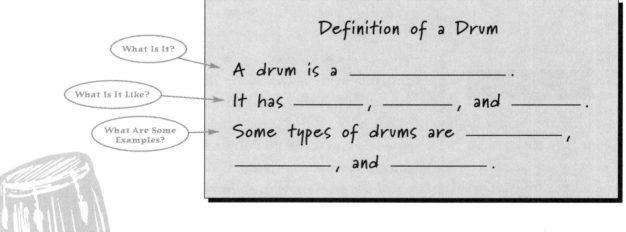

Definition of a Drum

What Is It? → A drum is a _____.

What Is It Like? → It has _____, _____, and _____.

What Are Some Examples? → Some types of drums are _____, _____, and _____.

Have students use the three categories of information (What Is It? What Is It Like? What Are Some Examples?) on the map to fill in the blanks and create a comprehensive definition of a drum. For example: *A drum is a percussion instrument. It has a hollow shell, a drumhead, and is played by striking with sticks or hands. Some types of drums are bass, conga, bongo, and snare.*

Guided Practice

Give students copies of "Marine Mammals" and then read aloud the selection. Ask: *How many of you think you know what marine mammals are? Can you tell me the general category to which marine mammals belong? Can you name any important characteristics of marine mammals? Can you name any examples of marine mammals?* Tell students that they are going to discover what they really know about marine mammals by filling in a Concept of Definition Map.

Give students copies of the Concept of Definition Map. Then use interactive whiteboard technology to display the map. Print the words *marine mammal* in the center box of the map and direct students to do the same. Ask students to reread the first sentence. Ask: *To what general category does a marine mammal belong?* (warm-blooded animal) Print *warm-blooded animal* in the box under the heading What Is It? and direct

CONCEPT OF DEFINITION MAP

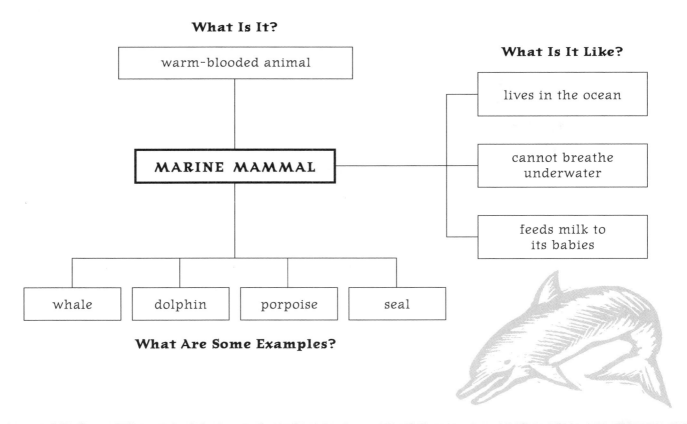

What Is It?

warm-blooded animal

What Is It Like?

lives in the ocean

MARINE MAMMAL

cannot breathe underwater

feeds milk to its babies

whale   dolphin   porpoise   seal

What Are Some Examples?

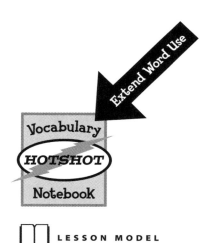

Vocabulary Hotshot Notebook, p. 189

students to do the same. Ask: *According to the selection, what are important characteristics of a marine mammal?* (Possible responses: *lives in the ocean, cannot breathe underwater*) Print *lives in the ocean* and *cannot breathe underwater* in two of the boxes under the heading What Is It Like? and direct students to do the same. Ask: *What is one type of marine mammal?* (a whale) Print *whale* in one of the boxes above the heading What Are Some Examples? and direct students to do the same.

Point out to students that the map for marine mammals is incomplete. To complete the map, they need to fill in one more box under What Is It Like? and to provide three more examples above the heading What Are Some Examples? Ask students to use a dictionary or other reference materials to complete the map. Students might suggest adding *feeds milk to its babies* under What Is It Like? and the examples *dolphins, porpoises,* and *seals.* After students have completed their maps, have them use the information on the map to write a definition of a marine mammal. For example: *A marine mammal is a warm-blooded animal. It lives in the ocean, cannot breathe underwater, and feeds milk to its babies. Some examples of a marine mammal are whales, dolphins, porpoises, and seals.*

Give students opportunities to share their maps and definitions, describe the process they used, and tell if what they know now about marine mammals differs from what they knew before.

Independent Practice

Provide students with another copy of the Concept of Definition Map so that they can explore other words or concepts they encounter in their reading. For example, students can choose words from authentic literature or content-area texts. Invite volunteers to discuss why they chose a particular target word and then share their maps and definitions.

LESSON MODEL FOR

Morphemic Analysis

Benchmark

• ability to use individual words in a compound word to derive its meaning

Grade Level

• Grade 2

Grouping

• whole class
• small group or pairs

Sample Text

• "Weekend Campout" (Resources)

Materials

• two clip art photos: a shoe and a box
• word cards *shoe, box, bee, hive, class, room, dog, house, fire, wood, home, work, rain, coat, wrist, watch*
• PDF of "Weekend Campout"
• dictionaries
• Vocabulary Hotshot Notebooks

Compound Words

The meaning of some compound words can be derived from the meanings of the two smaller words that comprise them: for example, *doghouse* and *bluebird.* Other compound words have a meaning that differs from the meaning of the two smaller words: for example, the word *butterfly.* This sample lesson model can be adapted and used to enhance vocabulary instruction in any commercial reading program.

Direct Explanation

Tell students that *shoebox* is a compound word—a word made up of two smaller words. Display the word cards *shoe* and *box* and have students read them aloud. Next, push or set the cards together to form the word *shoebox.* Have students say the new word and provide a simple definition; for example, "a box for shoes." Say: *The word* shoebox *is made up of two smaller words that can each stand alone. Knowing the meaning of each of the words in a compound word can help you figure out the meaning of the whole word.*

Teach/Model

Using interactive whiteboard technology, display the picture of a shoe. Say: *This is a shoe.* Print the word *shoe* below the picture. Remove the picture of the shoe and display the picture of a shoebox. Say: *This is a box.* Print the word *box* below the picture. Now show the picture of the shoe again. Move, or drag, the shoe inside the shoebox. Say: *Now, we have a shoebox.* Ask: *What is a shoebox?* (a box for shoes) Print the word *shoebox,* and say: *Now we have shoebox.*

110

Some compound words have a meaning that differs from the meaning of the two smaller words. Point out to students examples of these words, such as *butterfly* and *hotdog*.

Read the following sentences aloud, asking students to suggest the compound word that completes each sentence.

- A box for shoes is a _____. (shoebox)

- A fish that is gold is a _____. (goldfish)

- A boat that sails is a _____. (sailboat)

- A bird that is blue is a _____. (bluebird)

Display the following word cards in random order: *bee, hive, class, room, dog, house, fire, wood, home, work, rain, coat, wrist, watch.* Read the words aloud with students. Point out that each word has a meaning of its own, and that each can be used as part of a compound word. Have students suggest compound words that can be made from two of the word cards; as they suggest them, slide the two word cards together. Then invite volunteers to take turns making up incomplete sentences (like the ones above) for their classmates to complete. For example, they might suggest: *A house for a dog is a _____.*

Guided Practice

Use interactive whiteboard technology to display "Weekend Campout." Read the selection aloud, as students follow along with you. Then circle the following compound words: *weekend, backyard, campgrounds,* and *campsites.* Say: *These words are compound words. Sometimes you can figure out the meaning of a compound word if you know the meaning of the two smaller words.* Ask: *What are the two smaller words that make up the compound word* weekend? (*week* and *end*) Ask: *Based upon the meaning of the two smaller words, what is the meaning of* weekend? (the end of the week) Follow the same procedure for the other three words.

Compound Words	
weekend • end of a week	campgrounds • grounds on which to camp
backyard • yard in the back	campsites • sites or places on which to camp

Compound Words
birdcalls • calls of birds
breakfast • breaking the fast
trailhead • head of the trail
daypack • backpack for during the day
sweatshirts • shirts for sweat
uphill • up the hill
waterfall • place where water falls
riverbank • bank of a river
afternoon • after 12 o'clock noon
seashore • shore of the sea
sandcastles • castles made of sand
starfish • sea animal shaped like a star
dinnertime • time for dinner
sunset • setting of the sun
cookout • cooking food outdoors
campfire • fire built by campers
nighttime • time when it is night
overhead • over or above your head
weekend • end of the week
campouts • outdoor camping

Now circle the compound words *outdoors* and *outside*. Ask: *What are the two smaller words that make up the compound word* outdoors? (*out* and *doors*) Say: *The meaning of the compound word* outdoors *is different from the meaning of the two smaller words.* Outdoors *actually means "outside or in the open air," not "doors that go out." The same is true for* outside, *which actually means "in the open air."*

Independent Practice

Have pairs of students go through the remaining three paragraphs, finding and circling the compound words *birdcalls, breakfast, trailhead, daypack, sweatshirts, uphill, waterfall, riverbank, afternoon, seashore, sandcastles, starfish, dinnertime, sunset, cookout, campfire, hotdogs, nighttime, into, overhead, weekend,* and *campouts.* Remind students that some compound words have a meaning that differs from the meaning of the two smaller words, such as the words *hotdogs* and *into.* Then ask pairs to make a chart, like the one shown below, and use it to list each compound word, the two smaller words that make up the compound, and the meaning of the compound derived from the two smaller words. When students have finished, call on pairs to share information about the compound words they have found and listed on their charts.

111

COMPOUND WORD EVALUATION

Compound Word	Two Smaller Words	Meaning
trailhead	trail + head	the head of the trail

Morphemic Analysis

Benchmark

• ability to use concept of word families to derive the meanings of unfamiliar words

112

Grade Level

• Grade 2 and above

Prerequisite

• ability to identify root words

Grouping

• whole class
• small group or pairs

Materials

• dictionaries
• Vocabulary Hotshot Notebooks

Word Family

collect

collecting

collection

collector

Word Families

According to Nagy and Anderson (1984), a word family is a group of words related in meaning. For example, the words *add, addition, additive,* and *adding* belong to the same word family. Since words in a family all share the same root word, students who know the meaning of one of the words in a family can guess or infer the meanings of the others. This sample lesson model focuses on using knowledge about root words and word families to derive the meanings of unfamiliar words. The same model can be adapted and used to enhance morphemic analysis instruction in any commercial reading program.

Direct Explanation

Remind students that a root word is a single word that cannot be broken into smaller words or parts. Tell them that they can sometimes figure out the meaning of an unfamiliar word if they know the meaning of its root word. Explain that a group of words that has the same root word is called a word family and that words belonging to the same word family have related meanings. Point out to students that the word family *runner, running,* and *rerun* share the same root word, *run.* Explain to students that knowing about root words and word families can help them to figure out the meanings of unfamiliar words encountered in their reading.

Teach/Model

Print the word family *collect, collecting, collection,* and *collector* on the board and read it aloud. Say: *These words all belong to the same word family.* Collect, collecting, collection, *and* collector *all are formed from the root word* collect. Underline the root word *collect* in the words. Say: *If you collect things, you bring them together from several places. A collector is someone who finds things and brings them together, and a collection is a group of different but related things, such as a CD collection. I'm going to make up some sentences using words that share the root word* collect*: My friend likes collecting things. He is a collector of South American stamps. He keeps his collection in his desk.* Ask students to brainstorm different kinds of collections or collectors that they know about.

Guided Practice

Remind students that word families are words that share the same root word. Then print the following sentences on the board:

> Honestly, none of my friends are dishonest people. Honesty is something that I greatly respect. In my honest opinion, you cannot trust everyone.

HONEST

An honest person is someone who always tells the truth and does not cheat or break the law.

Word Family
hon<u>est</u>ly
dis<u>honest</u>
hon<u>est</u>y
<u>honest</u>

Read the sentences aloud. Ask: *Which words have the same root word?* (honestly, dishonest, honesty, honest) Say: *That's right, the words* honestly, dishonest, honesty, *and* honest *belong to the same word family.* Ask: *What is the root word?* (honest) Print the word family on the board and ask a volunteer to underline the root word *honest.* Then call on volunteers to explain the meaning of the root word *honest* and how the meanings of the other words in the family are closely related. For example, ask:

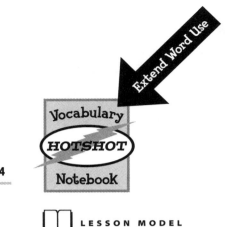

LESSON MODEL

Vocabulary Hotshot Notebook, p. 189

What are some examples of honesty? What are some examples of a lack of honesty, or dishonesty? (Answers will vary.) Then have students write sentences using words belonging to the *honest* word family. Provide an opportunity for students to share their sentences with the class.

Independent Practice

Challenge students to a Word Family Marathon. Give students 15 minutes to look through textbooks and other reading materials for words that are formed from root words. Have them make a list of the words on a worksheet, such as the one shown below. Then, for each word that they find, ask them to identify the root word and then brainstorm or use a dictionary to identify other words in the family. Have students each share one entry and explain how the meaning of the root word relates to the meaning of the other words in the family.

WORD FAMILY MARATHON

Word I Found	Root Word of Word I Found	Other Words in Family
disagree	agree	agreeable, agreeing, agrees, agreed, agreement

LESSON MODEL FOR

Morphemic Analysis

Benchmarks

- ability to identify the meaning of frequently used prefixes
- ability to derive word meanings from word-part clues

Grade Level

- Grade 3 and above

Grouping

- whole class
- small group or pairs
- individual

Sample Text

- "Marine Mammals" (Resources)

Materials

- chart paper
- PDF of "Marine Mammals"
- Vocabulary Hotshot Notebooks

Word-Part Clues: Prefixes

Graves (2004) defines prefixes as "elements that are attached to full English words." He suggests that beginning instruction in prefixes be restricted to common prefixes attached to Anglo-Saxon root words. Baumann et al. (2005) found that introducing affixes in groups or families helped students learn, recall, and apply them well. This sample lesson model targets prefixes *un–*, *in–*, and *im–*, which belong to the "Not" Prefix Family. The same model can be adapted and used to enhance word-part clue instruction in any commercial reading program.

Direct Explanation

Remind students that a root word is a single word that cannot be broken into smaller words or word parts and that a prefix is a word part added to the beginning of a root word that changes its meaning. Explain to students that since many root words have prefixes, it is useful to know how to look for and use these word parts to figure out the meanings of words. Caution them, however, that while this strategy is often useful, there are occasions when it does not work at all.

Teach/Model

Print the following information about the "Not" Prefix Family on the board:

> **"NOT" PREFIX FAMILY**
>
> un– <u>un</u>happy
> in– <u>in</u>visible
> im– <u>im</u>polite

Explain to students that families of prefixes have meanings in common. The prefixes *un–*, *in–*, and *im–* belong to the "Not" Prefix Family because they share the meaning of "not." Point out that *unhappy* means "not happy," *invisible* means "not visible," and *impolite* means "not polite."

116

Print the words *uncertain, unfair,* and *unwise* on the board and read them aloud. Say: *These words all begin with the prefix* un–, *a prefix belonging to the "Not" Prefix Family.* Point to the word *uncertain.* Say: *I'm going to show you how to use word-part clues to figure out what this word means. First I'll break the word into parts: prefix and root word.* Draw a slash between *un* and *certain.* Say: Uncertain *has two parts, the prefix* un– *and the root word* certain. *The root word* certain *means "sure." The prefix* un– *means "not." Now I'll put the meanings of the word parts together to get the meaning of the whole word. If* un– *means "not" and* certain *means "sure," then* uncertain *must mean "not sure" or "not certain."* Ask: *Who can tell me something they are uncertain about?* (Answers will vary.) Follow the same procedure for *unfair* and *unwise.*

Next print the words *inactive, incomplete,* and *injustice* on the board and read them aloud. Then follow the same teaching procedure as described above, pointing out that the prefix *in–* also belongs to the "Not" Prefix Family.

Finally, print the words *imperfect, immature,* and *improper* on the board and read them aloud. Then follow the same teaching procedure as described above, pointing out that the prefix *im–* also belongs to the "Not" Prefix Family.

POINT OUT LIMITATIONS   Explain to students that they must be careful when using this word-part clue strategy because it does not always work. Point out that sometimes the removal of letters that appear to be a prefix leaves no meaningful root word. Then provide the following three examples:

un/cle

in/dex

im/agine

un/easy

The most common meaning of the word *easy* is "simple or effortless." Removing the suffix *–y* from *easy* leaves the root word *ease. Ease* can be defined as "the state of feeling comfortable."

Print the word *uncle* on the board and read it aloud. Draw a slash between *un* and *cle* and then cover up the letters *un*. Say: *When I cover up the letters* un *in* uncle, *I am left with* cle, *which is not a meaningful root word. The letters* u *and* n *at the beginning of* uncle *do not function as a prefix.*

Print the word *index* on the board and read it aloud. Draw a slash between *in* and *dex* and then cover up the letters *in*. Say: *When I cover up the letters* in *in* index, *I am left with* dex, *which is not a meaningful root word. The letters* i *and* n *at the beginning of* index *do not function as a prefix.*

Print the word *imagine* on the board and read it aloud. Draw a slash between *im* and *agine* and then cover up the letters *im*. Say: *When I cover up the letters* im *in* imagine, *I am left with* agine, *which is not a meaningful root word. The letters* i *and* m *at the beginning of* imagine *do not function as a prefix.*

Now provide students with a different type of example. Print the word *uneasy* on the board and read it aloud. Draw a slash between *un* and *easy*. Say: *Sometimes, the combined meanings of a prefix and a root word do not help you to figure out the meaning of a whole word.* Uneasy *has two parts, the prefix* un– *and the root word* easy. *The prefix* un– *means "not." A common meaning of* easy *is "simple or effortless." But* uneasy *doesn't mean "not simple"; it actually means "uncomfortable or anxious." In this case, combining the meanings of the prefix* un– *and a common meaning of the root word* easy *doesn't result in the meaning of the whole word.*

WORD-PART CLUE EVALUATION

WORD	Does Not Have Prefix and Root Word	Has Prefix and Root Word	Prefix + Root Word = Meaning	Prefix + Root Word ≠ Meaning
unlike		un + like	not like	
impossible		im + possible	not possible	
indefinite		in + definite	not definite, unlimited	
uninterrupted		un + interrupted	not interrupted	
under	un + der			
impulse		im + pulse		sudden urge

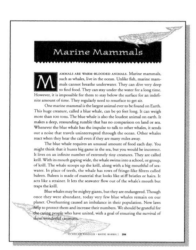

Guided Practice

Tell students that they are going to practice looking for words that appear to begin with "Not" Family Prefixes *un–, in–,* and *im–,* along with evaluating whether or not the letter groups are really prefixes and, if they are, whether or not using word-part clues is helpful in figuring out the meaning of the whole word. On chart paper, make a five-column Word-Part Clue Evaluation chart, such as the one shown above. Then read aloud and explain each of the column headings.

Use interactive whiteboard technology to display "Marine Mammals" and ask a volunteer to read aloud the first two paragraphs of the selection. Then guide students to identify the words in the sentences that may belong to the "Not" Prefix Family. On the chart, record the words *unlike, impossible, indefinite, uninterrupted, under,* and *impulse.* Next tell students that they are going to use the Word-Part Clue Evaluation chart to help them to analyze each of the listed words.

Point to the word *unlike* in the first paragraph of the selection. Say: *The word* unlike *begins with the letters* un, *which could be a prefix, so I'm going to try to break* unlike *into parts. I see the*

English/Spanish Cognates

impossible • imposible

impulse • impulso

root word like *and the prefix* un–, *so I'm going to print* un + like *in the third column of the chart under the heading Has Prefix and Root Word. Now I'll combine the meanings of the prefix* un– *and the root word* like. *I think* unlike *means "not like." To confirm, I'll substitute my meaning in the sentence: Not like fish, marine mammals can breathe underwater. Yes, "not like" makes sense. I'll print* not like *in the fourth column under the heading Prefix + Root Word = Meaning.*

Follow the same procedure for the words *impossible, indefinite,* and *uninterrupted.* All have prefixes and root words that are meaningful, so for these words the strategy works.

LIMITATIONS

un/der

LIMITATIONS Next, point to the word *under* in the first paragraph. Say: *The word* under *begins with the letters* un, *which could be a prefix, so I'm going to try to break the word into parts.* Ask: *Is* der *a meaningful word?* (no) *Do the letters* un *at the beginning of* under *function as a prefix?* (no) Say: *I'm going to print* un + der *in the second column of the chart under the heading Does Not Have Prefix and Root Word, to show that* under *does not have a prefix and a root word.*

im/pulse

Now point to the word *impulse* in the second paragraph. Say: *The word* impulse *begins with the letters* im, *which could be a prefix, so I'm going to try to break the word into parts. I see the root word* pulse, *so I'm going to print* im + pulse *in the third column under the heading Has Prefix and Root Word. Now I'll combine the meanings of the prefix* im– *and the root word* pulse. *The word* pulse *means "a regular beat," and the prefix* im– *means "not."* Ask: *When you combine these two meanings, what do you get?* ("not a regular beat") Say: *Right, I'm going to try out this meaning in the sentence: "Whenever the blue whale has not a regular beat to talk to other whales . . ."* Ask: *Does this meaning make sense in the sentence?* (no) Say: *That's right, the word* impulse *actually means "a sudden urge." Let's try this meaning in the sentence: "Whenever the blue whale has a sudden urge to talk to other*

Impulse **is a derivate of the word** *impel.* *Impel* **means "to be driven to do something."**

whales . . ." That makes sense! In this case, combining the meanings of the prefix im– *and the root word* pulse *did not result in the meaning of the whole word. For* impulse, *I'm going to print the phrase* sudden urge *in the last column under the heading* Prefix + Root Word ≠ Meaning.

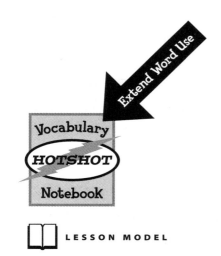

LESSON MODEL

Vocabulary Hotshot Notebook, p. 189

Independent Practice

Have students make a five-column chart, such as the one shown below. Have them copy the headings from the Word-Part Clue Evaluation chart onto their papers. Tell them that they are going to use the chart to finish the evaluation of possible prefixed words in "Marine Mammals." After students have completed their analysis, go over what they have found as a group. Encourage students to share their data and their rationale.

WORD-PART CLUE EVALUATION

WORD	Does Not Have Prefix and Root Word	Has Prefix and Root Word	Prefix + Root Word = Meaning	Prefix + Root Word ≠ Meaning
unusual		un + usual	not usual	
incorrect		in + correct	not correct	
infinite		in + finite	not finite, not limited	
imbalance		im + balance	not balanced, not equal in importance	
increase		in + crease		to become greater in number
united	un + ited			

LESSON MODEL FOR
Morphemic Analysis

Benchmarks

- ability to identify the meaning of derivational suffixes
- ability to derive word meanings from word-part clues

Grade Level

- Grade 3 and above

Grouping

- whole class
- small group or pairs
- individual

Sample Text

- "Marine Mammals" (Resources)

Materials

- chart paper
- PDF of "Marine Mammals"
- Vocabulary Hotshot Notebooks

SUFFIXES

cheer/ful
peace/ful
truth/ful
use/ful

Word-Part Clues: Suffixes

Researchers recommend that teachers spend time teaching derivational suffixes because, like prefixes, they are fairly regular in meaning and can lead to vocabulary expansion (Edwards et al. 2004). Common derivational suffixes include *–able, –ful, –less, –ness,* and *–or.* This sample lesson model targets the derivational suffix *–ful,* which is stable and obvious in meaning and thus easy for students to understand and apply to words. The same model can be adapted and used to enhance word-part clue instruction in any commercial reading program.

Direct Explanation

Remind students that a root word is a single word that cannot be broken into smaller words or word parts and that a suffix is a word part added to the end of a root word that changes its meaning. Explain to students that since many root words have suffixes, it is useful to know how to look for and use these word parts to figure out the meanings of words. Caution them, however, that while this strategy is often useful, there are occasions when it does not work at all.

Teach/Model

Print the words *cheerful, peaceful, truthful,* and *useful* on the board and read them aloud. Say: *These words all end with the suffix* –ful, *which means "full of."*

Point to the word *cheerful.* Say: *I'm going to show you how to use word-part clues to figure out what this word means. First I'll break the word into parts: root word and suffix.* Draw a slash between *cheer* and *ful.* Say: Cheerful *has two parts, the root word* cheer *and the suffix* –ful. *The root word* cheer *means "joy." The suffix* –ful *means "full of." Now I'll put the meanings of the word parts together to get the meaning of the whole word. If* cheer *means*

In *bashful,* the root word *bash* actually comes from the word *abash* which means "to make somebody feel ashamed, embarrassed, or uncomfortable."

"joy" *and* –ful *means "full of," then* cheerful *must mean "full of joy."* Ask: *Who can tell me why someone might be cheerful?* (Answers will vary.) Follow the same procedure for *peaceful, truthful,* and *useful.*

POINT OUT LIMITATIONS   Explain to students that they must be careful when using this strategy because it does not always work. Print the word *bashful* on the board and read it aloud. Draw a slash between *bash* and *ful.* Say: *Sometimes a root word is not obviously related in meaning to the whole word.* Say: Bashful *has two parts, the root word* bash *and the suffix* –ful. *The root word* bash *means "to smash something really hard." The suffix* –ful *means "full of." But the word* bashful *does not mean "full of a hard smash"; it actually means "uneasy in the presence of others." In this case, combining the meanings of the root word* bash *and the suffix* –ful *does not result in the meaning of the whole word.*

Guided Practice

Tell students that they are going to practice looking for words that end with the suffix *–ful,* along with evaluating whether or not using word-part clues is helpful in figuring out the meaning of the whole word. On chart paper, make a four-column Word-Part Clue Evaluation chart, such as the one shown below. Then read aloud and explain each of the column headings.

WORD-PART CLUE EVALUATION

WORD	Has Root Word and Suffix	Root Word + Suffix = Meaning	Root Word + Suffix ≠ Meaning
mouthful	mouth + ful	a full mouth	
wonderful	wonder + ful	full of wonder	
grateful	grate + ful		wanting to thank someone

Use interactive whiteboard technology to display "Marine Mammals" and ask a volunteer to read aloud the last two paragraphs of the selection. Then guide students to identify the words in the sentences that contain the suffix *–ful*. On the chart, record the words *mouthful, wonderful,* and *grateful.* Next, tell students that they are going to use the Word- Part Clue Evaluation chart to help them to analyze each of the listed words.

Point to the word *mouthful* in the third paragraph of the selection. Say: *The word* mouthful *ends with the letters* ful, *which could be a suffix, so I'm going to try to break* mouthful *into parts.* Ask: *Who can tell me the root word?* (mouth) *Who can tell me the suffix?* (ful) *The word* mouthful *has a root word and a suffix, so I am going to print* mouth + ful *in the second column of the chart under the heading Has Root Word and Suffix.* Say: *The suffix –*ful *can mean "full."* Ask: *When you combine the meanings of* mouth *and –*ful, *what do you get?* ("a full mouth") Say: *Right, I'm going to try the meaning in the sentence: "The whale scoops up the krill, along with a full mouth of sea water." That makes sense. So I'm going to print the phrase* a full mouth *in the third column under the heading Root Word + Suffix = Meaning.* Follow the same procedure for the word *wonderful* in the fourth paragraph of the selection.

CONTINUED ▷

mouth/ful
wonder/ful

The *grate* in *grateful* actually comes from the Latin root *grat* which means "thanks."

124

LIMITATIONS

grate/ful

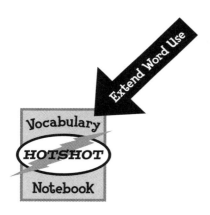

Vocabulary HOTSHOT Notebook

LESSON MODEL

Vocabulary Hotshot Notebook, p. 189

LIMITATIONS   Now point to the word *grateful* in the fourth paragraph. Say: *The word* grateful *ends with the letters* ful, *which could be a suffix, so I'm going to try to break* grateful *into parts. I see the root word* grate, *so I'm going to print* grate + ful *in the second column under the heading Has Root Word and Suffix. Now I'll combine the meanings of the root word and the suffix.* Ask: *What is a meaning of the root word* grate? ("a metal grid, like the one on a barbecue") *What is the meaning of the suffix* –ful? ("full of") Ask: *When you put together these two meanings, what do you get?* ("full of metal grid") Say: *Right, I'm going to try out this meaning in the sentence: "We should be full of metal grid for the caring people. . . ."* Ask: *Does this meaning make sense in the sentence?* (no) Say: *That's right, the word* grateful *actually means "wanting to thank someone." Let's try this meaning in the sentence: "We should want to thank the caring people. . . ." That makes sense! In this case, combining the meanings of the root word* grate *and the suffix* –ful *did not result in the meaning of the whole word. For* grateful, *I'm going to print the phrase* wanting to thank someone *in the last column under the heading Root Word + Prefix ≠ Meaning.*

Independent Practice

Have students fold lined sheets of paper lengthwise into fourths and then copy onto their paper the headings from the Word-Part Clue Evaluation chart. Tell students that they are going to use the chart to record and analyze words that end with the suffix –*ful.* Then direct them to look through their textbooks for words that end in the suffix –*ful.* After students have finished finding words and evaluating them, have the group share the words they have found along with their evaluations.

LESSON MODEL FOR
Morphemic Analysis

Benchmark

- ability to use knowledge of Greek roots to derive the meaning of unfamiliar words

Grade Level

- Grade 4 and above

Grouping

- whole class
- small group or pairs

Sample Text

- "Studying the Sky" (Resources)

Activity Master

- Word-Part Web (Resources)

Materials

- PDF and copies of Word-Part Web
- PDF of "Studying the Sky"
- dictionaries
- Vocabulary Hotshot Notebooks

tele + phone = telephone

Word-Part Clues: Roots

Students should understand that Greek and Latin roots are important meaning elements within words. It is useful to select roots from texts students are reading, choosing those that are most likely to occur again. Generally, Greek roots are introduced before Latin roots because their meanings are more apparent and the way in which they combine with other elements is more understandable. This sample lesson model focuses on knowledge of Greek roots to derive the meanings of unfamiliar words. The same strategy can be adapted and used to enhance morphemic analysis instruction in any commercial reading program.

Direct Explanation

Tell students that roots are word parts that come from the Greek and Latin languages. Explain that the difference between a root word and a root is that a root word, such as *play,* can stand alone as a word in English, but a root, such as *tele,* is not a word in English. Tell students that knowing about Greek roots can help them to figure out the meanings of unfamiliar words.

Teach/Model

Print the word *telephone* on the board and read it aloud. Tell students that they all know what a telephone is. Then explain to them that they may not know that the word *telephone* is made up of two Greek roots: *tele* and *phone.* Underline *tele* in *telephone.* Tell students that the Greek root *tele* means "distant or far away." Then print the following mathematical sentence on the board and read it aloud: *tele + phone = telephone.*

Say: *The other Greek root in* telephone *is* phone; *it means "sound." So if* tele *means "distant" and* phone *means "sound," the word* telephone *literally means "distant sound."* Ask: *Can anyone tell*

126

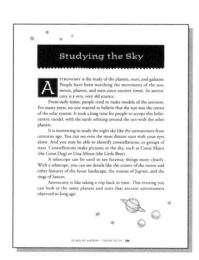

Point out to Spanish-speaking ELLs that *television* and *televisión* are identically spelled cognates.

me how this literal meaning of the word telephone *relates to the real-life function of a telephone?* (Possible response: *A telephone is equipment that is used to talk to someone in another, usually distant, place.*)

Next, print the word *television* on the board. Explain that the word *television* is made up of the root *tele* and the word *vision*. Underline *tele* in *televison*. Then print the following mathematical sentence on the board and read it aloud: *tele + vision = television.*

Say: Vision *is not a word of Greek origin. You may already know the meaning of the word* vision—*it has to do with "the ability to see something." So if* tele *means "distant," the word* television *literally means "distant vision."* Ask: *Can anyone tell me how this literal meaning of the word* television *relates to the real-life function of television?* (Possible response: *Television is a system of sending pictures, and sounds, over a distance so people can see them on a television set.*)

Use interactive whiteboard technology to display the Word-Part Web. Say: *I am going to begin a Word-Part Web for* tele. Print the word part *tele* in the middle oval. Say: *The words* telephone *and* television *both contain the root* tele. Then print these words in the web, as shown on the facing page.

Guided Practice

Use interactive whiteboard technology to display "Studying the Sky," highlighting the following sentence and underlining the word *telescope.*

A <u>telescope</u> can be used to see faraway things more clearly.

tele + scope =
telescope

English/Spanish Cognates

telegram • telegrama

telephone • teléfono

telescope • telescopio

SEE ALSO . . .

Common Greek and Latin Roots in

   English, p. 82

Print the word *telescope* on the board, underlining *tele.* Point to *tele* and ask: *What is the meaning of the root* tele? (distant or far away). Cover up *tele* and ask: *If I cover up* tele, *what is left?* (scope) Ask: *Who can print on the board a mathematical sentence for the word* telescope? Then ask a volunteer to read the mathematical sentence aloud: *tele + scope = telescope.*

Say: Scope *is another Greek root. It means "to view or to look at."* Ask: *So if* tele *means "distant or far away" and* scope *means "to view or look at," what is the literal meaning of the word* telescope? (Possible response: *to view or look at from a distance*) Ask: *Can anyone tell me how the literal meaning of the word* telescope *relates to the real-life function of a telescope?* (Possible response: *A telescope is an instrument that makes distant things seem larger and nearer when you look through it.*)

Display the partially completed Word-Part Web and say: *I am going to add the word* telescope *to our Word-Part Web.* Ask: *Can anyone think of another word having the word root* tele *that we could add to the web?* (Possible responses: *telecast, telegram, telesales*) Add students' suggestions to the web.

WORD-PART WEB

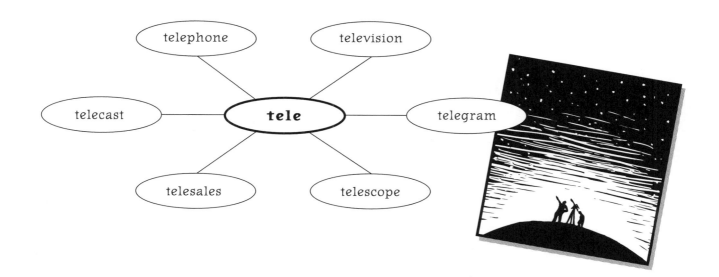

LESSON MODEL

Vocabulary Hotshot Notebook, p. 189

English/Spanish Cognates

chronoscope · cronoscopio

horoscope · horóscopo

kaleidoscope · caleidoscopio

microscope · microscopio

periscope · periscopio

stethoscope · estetoscopio

Independent Practice

Remind students that the Greek root *scope,* as in *telescope,* means "to view or to look at." Provide a copy of the Word-Part Web to pairs of students and ask them to construct a web for *scope.* Tell them that they should begin by printing the root *scope* in the center oval. Students should brainstorm and then record in the web all the words they can think of that have the root *scope* in them. (For example, *stethoscope, microscope, periscope, horoscope, kaleidoscope, chronoscope.*) After completing their webs, students should look up the definition of each unfamiliar word in the dictionary, explain the meaning of each word, and then tell how the root *scope* relates to that meaning.

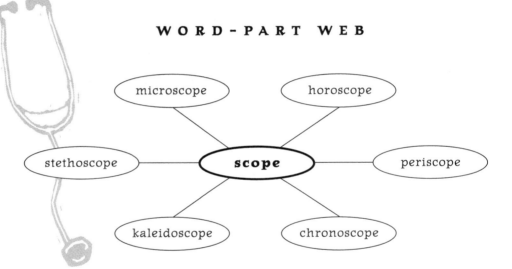

W O R D - P A R T   W E B

LESSON MODEL FOR
Contextual Analysis

Benchmark

• ability to use contextual analysis to infer word meanings

Grade Level

• Grade 2 and above

Grouping

• whole class
• small group or pairs
• individual

Sample Text

• "Weekend Campout" (Resources)

Materials

• chart paper
• PDF of "Weekend Campout"
• dictionaries
• Vocabulary Hotshot Notebooks

Context Clues

Directly teaching students how to use context clues to determine word meanings seems to be a logical—and critical—component of vocabulary instruction. Because students encounter such an enormous number of words as they read, even a small improvement in their ability to infer the meanings of unfamiliar words can result in a large number of words learned (Fukkink and de Glopper 1998). This sample lesson model can be adapted and used to enhance contextual analysis instruction in any commercial reading program.

129

Direct Explanation

Explain to students that context clues are words or phrases that give readers clues or ideas to the meaning of other words. Tell students that knowing about context clues may help to determine the meanings of unfamiliar words they may come across in their reading. Then print the following cloze sentence on the board and read it aloud: *They just delivered the sausage and cheese _____ that we ordered.*

> They just delivered the sausage and cheese
> _____ that we ordered.

Ask: *Who can guess the missing word in this sentence?* (pizza) *How did you know?* (Possible responses: *Pizzas come with sausage and cheese. Most pizza parlors deliver pizzas.*) *That's right. You just used the context clues in the sentence to correctly choose the missing word. The word* pizza *makes sense in the sentence:* They just delivered the sausage and cheese pizza that we ordered.

USING CONTEXT CLUES

When you come across an unfamiliar word in your reading:

1. Look for words or phrases that may be clues, or hints, to the word's meaning.

2. First, look for clues in the sentence that contains the word. Then, if you need to, look for clues in the sentences that come before or after.

3. Using the context clues, try to determine the meaning of the unfamiliar word.

4. Try out meaning in the original sentence, to check whether or not it makes sense.

When she fell off her bike, Nancy got a bruise on her knee that quickly turned black and blue.

Teach/Model

Display a copy of the Using Context Clues chart. Read the four steps aloud, briefly discussing each step. Tell students that much of the time they can use context clues to determine the meaning of an unfamiliar word in their reading.

Now print the following sentence on the board and read it aloud: *When she fell off her bike, Nancy got a bruise on her knee that quickly turned black and blue.*

Say: *I'm not sure about the meaning of the word* bruise. *I'm going to look for clues to help me determine its meaning. In the sentence, it says that Nancy fell off her bike. Nancy could have gotten hurt. I hurt myself the last time I fell off my bike. Maybe a bruise has something to do with being hurt.* Black and blue *is a really helpful clue. I know that if you are bumped really hard, an area of your skin will turn black and blue. I think a bruise is a black-and-blue mark on your skin that you get from being hurt. I'm going to try my meaning in the sentence to see how it works:* When she fell off her bike, Nancy got a black-and-blue mark on her knee. *That makes sense!*

When I answered the phone, I heard my sister's <u>agitated</u> voice.

POINT OUT LIMITATIONS   Say: *We were easily able to figure out the meaning of the word* bruise *using the context clues in the sentence. However, sometimes context doesn't help much. Some sentences don't provide enough information about the meaning of an unfamiliar word.* Print the following sentence on the board and read it aloud: *When I answered the phone, I heard my sister's agitated voice.*

Say: *This is an example of unhelpful context clues. I'm not sure about the meaning of* agitated *in this sentence, and I can't find any context clues to help me:* answered, phone, *and* voice *don't really help me. A number of possible meanings could make sense in this sentence, including "loud," "tiny," "quiet," "excited," "soft," "smooth," "frantic," or "boring," but the meaning of* agitated *is "very worried or upset." So, in this case, there are no context clues to help me.*

Guided Practice

Tell students that you are going to show them how to use context clues to figure out the meaning of an unfamiliar word that they may encounter in their reading. Use interactive whiteboard technology to display "Weekend Campout." Then ask a volunteer to read aloud the following sentences:

> **The path leads sharply uphill to a waterfall. It is a <u>steep</u> climb!**

CONTEXT CLUES

Target Word

steep

Underline the word *steep* in blue. Say: *I'm not sure about the meaning of the word* steep. *So I am going to ask you to help me look for clues to its meaning.* Ask: *Can anyone find a context clue in the second sentence?* (*Climb* may be a clue.) Underline the word *climb* in green. Ask: *Does the word* climb *provide enough information for you to figure out the meaning of* steep? (no) *Where can you look if you need more clues?* (in the first sentence) *Are there any context clues in the first sentence?*

(sharply, uphill) Underline the words *sharply* and *uphill* in green. Say: *Let's put together the clues that we found and try to determine a meaning for* steep. *When you climb, you go upward or uphill. A steep climb may be one that goes up a hill that has a sharp slant, or is almost straight up and down.* Steep *may mean something like "a slant that is almost straight up and down." You've got to be in good shape to climb a steep hill.* Ask: *Who wants to try our meaning for* steep *in the sentence to see if it fits?* (It is an almost straight-up-and-down climb!) Say: *That makes sense, so for now we'll assume that* steep *refers to the up-and-down slant of a hill.*

Target Words

devour
plummet

LESSON MODEL

Vocabulary Hotshot Notebook, p. 189

Independent Practice

In "Weekend Campout," underline the words *devour* and *plummet* in blue. Ask a volunteer to read aloud the next two sentences:

> They hungrily <u>**devour**</u> their lunch by the riverbank. From the rocks, Fay can watch the water <u>**plummet**</u> over the cliff.

Ask pairs of students to follow the steps on the Using Context Clues chart to figure out the meanings for *devour* and *plummet*. Have them share their context clues, meanings, and the process they used to arrive at the meanings. Then have them look up the words in a dictionary to confirm the meanings. (Possible meanings: Devour *means "to eat quickly and eagerly."* Plummet *means "to drop steeply and suddenly downward."*)

LESSON MODEL FOR

Contextual Analysis

Benchmarks

- ability to recognize types of semantic context clues
- ability to use context clues to infer word meanings

Grade Level

- Grade 4 and above

Prerequisite

- Context Clues

Grouping

- whole class
- small group or pairs
- individual

Teaching Chart

- Types of Helpful Context Clues (Resources)

Materials

- copies of Types of Helpful Context Clues chart

DEFINITION CLUES

Target Word

conga

Introducing Types of Context Clues

Instruction in specific types of context clues is an effective approach for teaching students to use context to infer word meanings (Fukkink and de Glopper 1998). Baumann and his colleagues (2002, 2003) recommend teaching five types of context clues: definition, synonym, antonym, example, and general. This sample lesson model can be adapted and used to enhance contextual analysis instruction in any commercial reading program.

Direct Explanation

Tell students that they can sometimes use context clues to figure out the meaning of an unfamiliar word they come across in their reading. Remind them that context clues are the words, phrases, and sentences surrounding an unfamiliar word that can give hints or clues to its meaning. Caution students that although these clues can prove to be helpful, they can sometimes be misleading.

Teach/Model

Give students copies of the Types of Helpful Context Clues chart. Briefly go over the chart, identifying the types of context clues and discussing the example for each one. Tell students that they should refer to the chart as they learn more about the five different types of context clues.

Definition Context Clues

Explain to students that in a definition clue the author provides the reader with the specific definition, or meaning, of a word right in the sentence. Point out that words such as *are, is, means,* and *refers to* can signal that a definition clue may follow. Then print the following sentences on a transparency:

English/Spanish Cognate

conga • conga

134

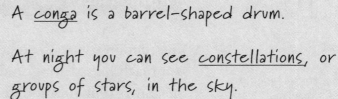

A <u>conga</u> is a barrel-shaped drum.

At night you can see <u>constellations</u>, or groups of stars, in the sky.

Read aloud the first sentence. Say: *I'm going to look for a context clue to help me understand the meaning of the word* conga. Underline *conga* in blue. Say: *In the sentence, I see the word* is. *The word* is *can signal a definition context clue.* Underline *is* in red. Say: *The phrase* a barrel-shaped drum *follows the word* is. Underline the context clue in green. Say: *A conga is a barrel-shaped drum. The author has given a definition context clue.*

TYPES OF HELPFUL CONTEXT CLUES

Type	Description	Example Sentence
Definition	The author provides a direct definition of an unfamiliar word, right in the sentence. • SIGNAL WORDS: *is, are, means, refers to*	A <u>conga</u> *is* a barrel-shaped drum.
Appositive Definition	A type of definition clue. An appositive is a word or phrase that defines or explains an unfamiliar word that comes before it. • SIGNAL WORD: *or* • SIGNAL PUNCTUATION: set off by commas	At night you can see <u>constellations</u>, *or* groups of stars, in the sky.
Synonym	The author uses another word or phrase that is similar in meaning, or can be compared, to an unfamiliar word. • SIGNAL WORDS: *also, as, identical, like, likewise, resembling, same, similarly, too*	My dog Buck travels everywhere with me. My friend's <u>canine</u> buddy travels everywhere with him, *too.*
Antonym	The author uses another word or phrase that means about the opposite of, or is in contrast with, an unfamiliar word. • SIGNAL WORDS: *but, however, in contrast, instead of, on the other hand, though, unlike*	I thought the movie would be weird, *but* it turned out to be totally <u>mundane</u>.
Example	The author provides several words or ideas that are examples of an unfamiliar word. • SIGNAL WORDS: *for example, for instance, including, like, such as*	In science we are studying <u>marine mammals</u> *such as* whales, dolphins, and porpoises.
General	The author provides some nonspecific clues to the meaning of an unfamiliar word, often spread over several sentences.	Einstein rode his bike everywhere. He thought driving a car was way too <u>complicated</u>.

Based on Baumann et al. 2003, 2005.

Target Word

constellations

English/Spanish Cognate

constellation • constelación

APPOSITIVE DEFINITION CLUE Explain to students that sometimes a definition clue is set off in a sentence by commas, and that this type of definition clue is called an appositive definition clue. Tell them that an appositive is a word or phrase that defines or explains a word that comes before it. Point out that appositives may include a signal word such as *or*.

Read aloud the second sentence. Say: *I'm going to look for a context clue to help me understand the meaning of the word* constellations. Underline *constellations* in blue. Say: *In the middle of the sentence, following the word* constellations, *there is a phrase set off by commas. Commas and the word* or *can signal an appositive definition clue.* Underline the commas and the word *or* in red. Say: *The phrase* or groups of stars *is an appositive definition clue.* Underline the appositive definition clue in green. Say: *A constellation is a group of stars. The author has given an appositive definition clue.*

Target Word

canine

English/Spanish Cognate

canine • canino

Synonym Context Clues

Remind students that a synonym is a word that has the same, or almost the same, meaning as another word. Explain that in a synonym context clue the author uses a familiar word or phrase in a sentence or nearby sentence that is similar in meaning, or can be compared, to the word they are trying to understand. Point out that words such as *also, as, identical, like, resembling, same, similarly,* and *too* can signal a synonym context clue. Then display the following sentences:

> My dog Buck travels everywhere with me. My friend's <u>canine</u> buddy travels everywhere with him, too.

136

Read aloud the two sentences. Say: *I'm going to look for a context clue to help me understand the meaning of the word* canine. Underline *canine* in blue. Say: *At the end of the second sentence, I see the word* too. Too *can signal a synonym context clue.* Underline *too* in red. Say: *The first sentence tells about a dog, my dog Buck, who travels everywhere with me. The next sentence tells about my friend's canine buddy who travels everywhere with him. I know the word* buddy *means "friend" and that a dog is often called "man's best friend." So I'm going to guess that the word* canine *has something to do with dogs.* Dog *is a synonym context clue for* canine. Underline *dog* in green. Say: *The word* canine *means "relating to a dog." The author has given a synonym context clue.*

Antonym Context Clues

Remind students that an antonym is a word or phrase that means the opposite of another word. Explain that in an antonym context clue the author uses a familiar word or phrase in a sentence or nearby sentence that is the opposite in meaning to, or can be contrasted with, the word they are trying to understand. Point out to students that words such as *but, however, in contrast, instead of, on the other hand, though,* and *unlike* can signal an antonym context clue. Then display the following sentence:

> I thought the movie would be weird, but it turned out to be totally <u>mundane.</u>

Read the sentence aloud. Say: *I'm going to look for a context clue to help me understand the meaning of the word* mundane. Underline *mundane* in blue. Say: *In the middle of the sentence, I see the word* but. *The word* but *can signal an antonym context clue.* Underline *but* in red. Say: *I think the word* weird *may mean the opposite of* mundane. Underline *weird* in green. Say:

Everybody knows that weird *means "strange or unusual." Something that is the opposite of* weird *is something that is ordinary or commonplace. So I'm going to guess that the word* mundane *means "ordinary." In the sentence, I'm going to substitute the word* ordinary *for the word* mundane: "*I thought the movie would be weird, but it turned out to be totally ordinary." That makes sense! The author has given an antonym context clue.*

EXAMPLE CLUES

Target Term

marine
mammals

Example Context Clues

Explain to students that in an example context clue the author names things in the sentence or nearby sentences that belong to the same category as, or are examples of, the word they are trying to understand. Point out that words such as *for example, for instance, including, like,* and *such as* can signal an example context clue. Then display the following sentence:

> In science we are studying <u>marine mammals</u> such as whales, dolphins, and porpoises.

Read aloud the sentence. Say: *I'm going to look for a context clue to help me understand the meaning of the term* marine mammals. Underline *marine mammals* in blue. Say: *In the sentence, I see the words* such as. Such as *can signal an example context clue.* Underline *such as* in red. Say: *In the sentence, I see a familiar animal name. A whale is one example of a marine mammal. Dolphins and porpoises are other examples.* Underline the example context clues in green. Say: *The author has provided example context clues.*

GENERAL CLUES

Target Word

complicated

138

English/Spanish Cognate

complicated · complicado

General Context Clues

Remind students that the context in which an unfamiliar word appears often—but not always—contains specific clues to the word's meaning. Explain that sometimes the author provides only general context clues to the meaning of an unfamiliar word, and that these clues are often spread over several sentences or a paragraph. In this case, students can use details in the words or sentences surrounding the unfamiliar word, along with their prior knowledge and experience, to infer the meaning of the unfamiliar word. Then display the following sentences:

> Einstein rode his bike everywhere. He thought driving a car was way too complicated.

Read aloud the two sentences. Say: *I'm going to look for general context clues to help me understand the meaning of the word* complicated. Underline *complicated* in blue. Say: *To ride a bicycle, you have to know how to pedal, brake, and steer. A bike doesn't have a motor. To drive a car, though, you need to know how to fill it with gas, how to back up and park, and what to do if it breaks down. It's a lot harder to drive a car than a bike. I think* complicated *has something to do with being hard to do. In the sentence, I'm going to substitute the word* hard *for the word* complicated*: "He thought driving a car was way too hard." That makes sense. Now, I'm going to check the dictionary to be sure. According to the dictionary, something that is complicated has many parts and is therefore difficult to understand. Hard to do and difficult to understand are close in meaning. The author has given only general context clues. So using what I knew about driving helped me to figure out the meaning of the word* complicated.

LESSON MODEL FOR

Contextual Analysis

Benchmarks

• ability to recognize types of semantic context clues
• ability to use context clues to infer word meanings

Grade Level

• Grade 4 and above

Prerequisite

• Introducing Types of Context Clues

Grouping

• whole class
• small group or pairs
• individual

Sample Text

• "Percussion Instruments" (Resources)

Teaching Chart

• Types of Helpful Context Clues (Resources)

Materials

• PDF of "Percussion Instruments"
• lined paper
• Vocabulary Hotshot Notebooks

Applying Types of Context Clues

This is the second part of the Types of Context Clues lesson model. These sample lesson models can be used to enhance contextual analysis instruction in any commercial reading program.

Direct Explanation

Tell students that they are going to practice using what they know about types of context clues to figure out the meanings of some possibly unfamiliar words. Remind students that they may find it useful to refer to the Types of Helpful Context Clues chart.

Guided Practice

Use interactive whiteboard technology to display the first page of "Percussion Instruments," underlining the following target words in blue: *percussion instrument, percussion instruments, prevalent,* and *differ.*

A **percussion instrument** is any musical instrument that you play by striking or hitting using either sticks or your hands. There are many kinds of **percussion instruments**, including drums, cymbals, and xylophones. Of all the percussion instruments, drums are the most **prevalent**. They are commonly found all over the world. The drums may **differ** from culture to culture, place to place, and group to group, but all of them possess the same basic elements.

DEFINITION CLUES

Target Term

percussion instrument

A <u>percussion instrument</u> is any musical instrument that you play by striking or hitting using either sticks or your hands.

140

After asking a volunteer to read aloud the first sentence, say: *Let's try to figure out the meaning of the term* percussion instrument. Ask: *Are there any signal words in the sentence?* (yes, *is*) Underline *is* in red. Ask: *What type of context clue might we look for?* (definition clue) Say: *Right.* Ask: *What is a percussion instrument?* ("any musical instrument that you play by striking or hitting using either sticks or your hands") Underline the definition clue in green. Ask: *Where did you find the definition context clue?* (right in the sentence) Now ask a volunteer to read aloud the second sentence:

EXAMPLE CLUES

Target Term

percussion instruments

There are many kinds of <u>percussion instruments</u>, including drums, cymbals, and xylophones.

English/Spanish Cognates

percussion • percusión

instruments • instrumentos

Say: *This sentence tells us more about percussion instruments.* Ask: *Is there a signal word in the sentence?* (yes, *including*) Underline *including* in red. Ask: *What type of context clue might we look for?* (example clue) Say: *Right.* Ask: *Does the sentence give some examples of percussion instruments?* (yes, *drums, cymbals,* and *xylophones*) Underline the example clues in green. Say: *That's right.* Drums, cymbals, *and* xylophones *are examples of percussion instruments.* Now ask a volunteer to read aloud the next two sentences:

SYNONYM CLUES

Target Word

prevalent

Of all the percussion instruments, drums are the most <u>prevalent</u>. They are commonly found all over the world.

Say: *The unfamiliar word in the first sentence is* prevalent. Ask: *Can you find a signal word in these sentences?* (no) Say: *That's right, there are not always signal words to help us.* Ask: *Can you find a word or phrase in either one of the sentences that could be a synonym context clue?* (yes, *commonly found*) Underline the synonym clue in green. Say: *Yes,* prevalent *and* commonly found *have similar meanings.* Prevalent *means "very common."* Ask: *Who can substitute* very common *for the most* prevalent *to see if it makes sense?* Have the volunteer make the substitution and repeat the sentences. Now ask a volunteer to read aloud the next sentence:

ANTONYM CLUES

Target Word

differ

The drums may <u>differ</u> from culture to culture, place to place, and group to group, but all of them possess the same basic elements.

Say: *The unfamiliar word in the sentence is* differ. Ask: *Can you find a signal word in the sentence?* (yes, *but*) Underline *but* in red. Ask: *What kind of context clue might we look for?* (an antonym clue) Ask: *Can you find a word or phrase in the sentence that may mean the opposite of* differ*?* (yes, *same*) Underline the antonym clue in green. Ask: *Why did you choose* same*?* (Possible response: Differ *reminds me of the word* different *and I know that* same *and* different *are opposites.*) Say: *Right, if things differ, it means that they are "not like each other." The word* differ *means almost the opposite of the word* same. Ask: *Who can substitute the phrase* are not like each other *for the phrase* may differ *to see if it makes sense?* Have the volunteer make the substitution and repeat the sentence.

C O N T E X T   C L U E   E V A L U A T I O N

Unfamiliar Word	Signal Word or Punctuation	Context Clue	Type of Context Clue
amplify	or, comma	make it louder	appositive, definition
faint	compared to	huge noise	antonym
hide	or, commas	skin	synonym
vibrates	or	moves very quickly back and forth	definition
resonant	or, commas	deep and rich	synonym
rhythms	none	beating hearts	general

English/Spanish Cognates

amplify · amplificar

vibrate · vibrar

resonant · resonante

rhythms · ritmos

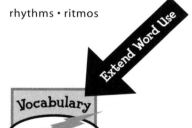

 **LESSON MODEL**

Vocabulary Hotshot Notebook, p. 189

Independent Practice

In "Percussion Instruments," underline the following target words in blue: *amplify, faint, hide, vibrates, resonant,* and *rhythms.* Tell students that they are going to practice using different types of context clues to figure out the meaning of the underlined words.

Then have students fold lined paper lengthwise in fourths and copy onto their papers the headings from the Context Clue Evaluation chart shown above. Have students work in pairs to complete the chart. After students have completed their analysis, go over what they have found together. Encourage students to think aloud as they share their process, choices, and rationale. An example of a completed chart is shown above.

143

LESSON MODEL FOR
Combined Morphemic & Contextual Analysis

Benchmark

- ability to use a combination of contextual and morphemic analysis to figure out word meanings

Grade Level

- Grade 4 and above

Prerequisites

- Word-Part Clues: Prefixes
- Word-Part Clues: Suffixes
- Context Clues
- Types of Context Clues

Grouping

- whole class
- small group or pairs
- individual

Teaching Charts

- The Vocabulary Strategy (Resources)
- Types of Helpful Context Clues (Resources)

Materials

- chart paper
- dictionaries
- Vocabulary Hotshot Notebooks

Introducing The Vocabulary Strategy

The Vocabulary Strategy is an adaptation of the Vocabulary Rule, a teaching strategy employed in two recent studies by Baumann et al. (2002, 2003, 2005). When encountering unfamiliar words in their reading, students can expand their vocabularies by knowing when to use contextual analysis (e.g., context clues), when to use morphemic analysis (e.g., word-part clues), and when to use both strategies in combination. The Vocabulary Strategy is presented in two parts: introducing the strategy and practicing the strategy. These sample lesson models can be used to enhance word-learning strategy instruction in any commercial reading program.

Direct Explanation

Remind students of the word-part and context-clue strategies they have already learned. Display a copy of The Vocabulary Strategy chart on the following page. Explain to students that The Vocabulary Strategy is a strategy for figuring out the meaning of an unfamiliar word by using context and word-part clues in combination. Then read the five steps of the strategy aloud, briefly explaining how each step functions. Point out to students that sometimes The Vocabulary Strategy cannot be fully applied—the surrounding text does not always contain useful context clues and some words cannot be divided into smaller parts.

THE VOCABULARY STRATEGY

To figure out the meaning of an unfamiliar word that you come across while reading:

1. Look for Context Clues in the Words, Phrases, and Sentences Surrounding the Unfamiliar Word

2. Look for Word-Part Clues Within the Unfamiliar Word
   A. Try to Break the Word into Parts. (If you can't, skip to Step 3.)
   B. Look at the Root Word. What does it mean?
   C. Look at the Prefix. What does it mean?
   D. Look at the Suffix. What does it mean?
   E. Put the Meanings of the Word Parts Together. What is the meaning of the whole word?

3. Guess the Word's Meaning (Use Steps 1 and 2.)

4. Try Out Your Meaning in the Original Sentence to Check Whether or Not It Makes Sense in Context

5. Use the Dictionary, if Necessary, to Confirm Your Meaning

Based on Baumann et al. 2003, 2005.

VOCABULARY STRATEGY

Target Words

cramped
uncomfortable
trudged

Print the following social-studies text excerpt on chart paper, and ask a volunteer to read it aloud. Tell students that today they will learn how to use The Vocabulary Strategy to figure out the meanings of the words *cramped, uncomfortable,* and *trudged.*

A wagon train on the move could be one mile long and one mile wide. Bumping along inside a <u>cramped</u> wagon was a hard and <u>uncomfortable</u> way to travel. Pioneers often <u>trudged</u> beside the wagons instead. Consequently, most people walked slowly all the way to Oregon—nearly two thousand miles.

VOCABULARY STRATEGY

Target Word

uncomfortable

A wagon train on the move could be one mile long and one mile wide. Bumping along inside a cramped wagon was a hard and <u>uncomfortable</u> way to travel.

LESSON MODELS

Context Clues, p. 129

Word-Part Clues: Prefixes, p. 115

Word-Part Clues: Suffixes, p. 121

Teach/Model—Context and Word-Part Clues

▶ 1. Look for Context Clues

In the excerpt, point to the word *uncomfortable.* Say: *I'm going to use The Vocabulary Strategy to figure out the meaning of* uncomfortable. *Step 1 says to look for context clues. I'm going to read the words, phrases, and sentences surrounding* uncomfortable *to see if I can find any context clues.* Read aloud the second sentence. Say: *The phrase* bumping along *and the word* hard *may be context clues. Riding down a bumpy road really bothers me; it can be rough on your body.* Hard *means "very difficult." I wonder if* uncomfortable *describes how it feels when something is rough or bothersome to your body.*

▶ 2A. Look for Word-Part Clues—Try to Break the Word into Parts

Say: *Now we are going to look for word-part clues. Step 2A tells me to try to break the word into parts. I see that I can break* uncomfortable *into three word parts: prefix* un–, *root word* comfort, *and suffix* –able. *If I can figure out what the parts mean and then put the word back together, I will get the meaning of the whole word.*

▶ 2B. Look for Word-Part Clues—Look at the Root Word

Say: *Step 2B says to look at the root word of* uncomfortable. *The root word is a single word that cannot be broken into smaller words or parts. The root word of* uncomfortable *is* comfort. *I think that* comfort *means "when your body feels relaxed"—such as the way it feels when you are napping on a pile of fluffy pillows.*

CONTINUED ▷

VOCABULARY STRATEGY

Target Word

uncomfortable

un/comfort/able

ROOT WORD

a single word that cannot be broken into smaller words or parts

PREFIX

a word part added to the beginning of a root word that changes its meaning

SUFFIX

a word part added to the end of a root word that changes its meaning

▶ **2C. Look for Word-Part Clues—Look at the Prefix**

Say: *Step 2C says to look at the prefix.* Say: *I see the prefix* un–. *The prefix* un– *means "not or opposite of." If I put the prefix* un– *and the root word* comfort *together, I get the word* uncomfort. Uncomfort *may mean "when your body doesn't feel relaxed."*

▶ **2D. Look for Word-Part Clues—Look at the Suffix**

Say: *Step 2D says to look at the suffix.* Say: *I see the suffix* –able. *The suffix* –able *means "able to or can be done."*

▶ **2E. Look for Word-Part Clues—
      Put the Meanings of the Word Parts Together**

Say: *Step 2E says to put the meanings of the root word and any prefix or suffix together to build the meaning of the whole word. If* un– *means "not," and* comfort *means "when your body feels relaxed,"* uncomfort *means "when your body does not feel relaxed." Then, if* –able *means "able to," then* uncomfortable *may mean "when your body is not able to feel relaxed."*

▶ **3. Guess the Word's Meaning**

Say: *Now let's go to Step 3. It says to use what I inferred from context clues in Step 1 and what I derived from word-part clues in Step 2 to guess, or speculate about, the meaning of* uncomfortable. *I think that* uncomfortable *might mean "not very relaxing, or rough on my body."*

▶ **4. Try Out Your Meaning in the Original Sentence**

Say: *Now let's go to Step 4. It tells me to try out my meaning in the original sentence, to see whether or not it makes sense in context. I am going to substitute* not very relaxing, or rough on my body *for the word* uncomfortable. *"Bumping along inside a cramped wagon was a hard and not very relaxing, or rough on my body way to travel." Yes, that makes sense. Your body can't be relaxed when it is being bumped up and down.*

> ▶ **5. Use the Dictionary**

Say: *Step 5 tells me to use the dictionary to confirm the meaning of* uncomfortable. Say: *The dictionary says that* uncomfortable *means "feeling a lack of or not providing physical comfort." My guess based on context clues and word-part clues was close.*

Conclude by saying: *Each step of The Vocabulary Strategy helps us to get closer to the meaning of an unfamiliar word. Together, the five steps of The Vocabulary Strategy helped us understand the meaning of the word* uncomfortable.

147

📖 **LESSON MODELS**

Using the Dictionary, p. 94

Introducing Types of Context Clues, p. 133

VOCABULARY STRATEGY

Target Word

trudged

Pioneers often trudged beside the wagons instead. Consequently, most people walked slowly all the way to Oregon—nearly two thousand miles.

Teach/Model—Context Clues Only

Tell students that sometimes they have to skip steps of The Vocabulary Strategy, as in the next example, where there are no word-part clues to rely on.

> ▶ **1. Look for Context Clues**

Display the Types of Helpful Context Clues chart. Say: *I am going to use this chart to help me to figure out the meaning of* trudged. *Step 1 of The Vocabulary Strategy tells me to look for context clues.* Say: *I can't find any context clues in the third sentence "Pioneers often trudged beside the wagons instead," so I am going to look for clues in the next sentence, "Consequently, most people walked slowly all the way to Oregon—nearly two thousand miles." I think I may have found a synonym clue for* trudged, *the phrase "walked slowly."* Trudged *might mean almost the same as "walked slowly."*

CONTINUED ▷

VOCABULARY STRATEGY

Target Word

trudged

148

Point out to Spanish-speaking ELLs that *pioneer* and *pionero* are cognates.

▶ **2A. Look for Word-Part Clues—Try to Break the Word into Parts**

Say: *Now let's go to Step 2. Step 2A says to try to break the word into parts. In* trudged, *I see the ending –ed, which tells me that the word is in the past tense, but I don't see a meaningful prefix or suffix. So I'll skip down to Step 3.*

▶ **3. Guess the Word's Meaning**

Say: *Step 3 says to use the context clues I found in Step 1 to guess the meaning of the word. I think trudging may be a way of walking—walking slowly.*

▶ **4. Try Out Your Meaning in the Original Sentence**

Say: *Now let's go to Step 4. It tells me to try out my meaning in the original sentence, to see whether or not it makes sense in context. I am going to substitute* walked slowly *for* trudged. *"Pioneers often walked slowly beside the wagons instead." In other words, instead of riding in the wagons, the pioneers walked slowly beside them. That makes sense.*

▶ **5. Use the Dictionary**

Say: *Step 5 tells me to use the dictionary to confirm the meaning of* trudged. *The dictionary says that* to trudge *is "to walk with slow, heavy steps." My guess from the use of context was close, but I didn't get the part about "heavy steps." That make sense. The pioneers must have been really tired. I walk that way when I'm tired, especially at the end of a long hike.*

VOCABULARY STRATEGY
Target Word
cramped
Bumping along inside a <u>cramped</u> wagon was a hard and uncomfortable way to travel.

Teach/Model—Nondirective Context Clues Only

Tell students that The Vocabulary Strategy doesn't always work well. Sometimes a word has no word-part clues and the context clues are limited. In those cases, the best you can do is to make a general guess about what a word means.

▶ 1. Look for Context Clues

Say: *I am going to try to use The Vocabulary Strategy to figure out the meaning of the word* cramped. *Step 1 tells me to look for context clues. I can tell that* cramped *is an adjective that describes the word* wagon, *but I can't really find any other context clues that help me to guess what it means. With such limited context, there are a number of possible meanings for the word* cramped *that would make sense in the sentence. The words* closed, little, hot, *and* old *are all adjectives that could describe the wagon.*

▶ 2A. Look for Word-Part Clues—Try to Break the Word into Parts

Say: *Now let's go to Step 2 of The Vocabulary Strategy. Step 2A says to try to break the word into parts. In* cramped, *I see the ending* –ed, *which tells me that the word is in the past tense, but I don't see a meaningful prefix or suffix. I'll have to skip down to Step 5 and look up* cramped *in the dictionary.*

▶ 5. Use the Dictionary

Say: *Step 5 tells me to use the dictionary. The dictionary says that* cramped *means "uncomfortably small or overcrowded." That makes sense. The pioneers were uncomfortable because they were crowded into too small a space. The wagons must have been tightly packed with family possessions; the wagons were too small for all the things the pioneers had to bring with them.*

TEACHER NOTE

Remember this lesson model is presented in two parts. The second part, Practicing The Vocabulary Strategy, begins on page 150.

LESSON MODEL FOR
Combined Morphemic & Contextual Analysis

Benchmark

• ability to use a combination of contextual and morphemic analysis to figure out word meanings

Grade Level

• Grade 4 and above

Prerequisites

• Introducing The Vocabulary Strategy

Grouping

• whole class
• small group or pairs
• individual

Activity Master

• The Vocabulary Strategy Worksheet (Resources)

Teaching Charts

• The Vocabulary Strategy (Resources)
• Types of Helpful Context Clues (Resources)

Materials

• chart paper
• PDF and copies of The Vocabulary Strategy Worksheet
• dictionaries
• Vocabulary Hotshot Notebooks

Practicing The Vocabulary Strategy

This is the second part of The Vocabulary Strategy lesson. These sample lesson models can be used to enhance word-learning strategy instruction in any commercial reading program.

Direct Explanation

Display a copy of The Vocabulary Strategy chart and the Types of Helpful Context Clues chart. Print the following science text excerpt on chart paper, and ask a volunteer to read it aloud.

> **The blue whale is the loudest animal on earth. The noise it makes is <u>incomparable</u> on land or sea; it is one of a kind. Whenever the blue whale wants to talk to other whales, it sends out a long, deep <u>rumble</u>. Whales many miles away can hear the sound.**

VOCABULARY STRATEGY

Target Words

incomparable
rumble

Give students two copies of The Vocabulary Strategy Worksheet. Tell them that today they will learn how to use The Vocabulary Strategy and The Vocabulary Strategy Worksheet to figure out the meanings of the words *incomparable* and *rumble*. Explain that you are going to guide them through the procedure for filling out the worksheet, helping them to apply the five steps of The Vocabulary Strategy.

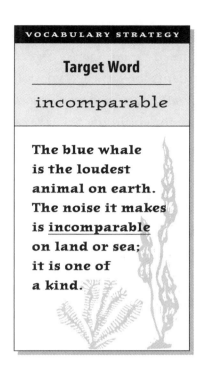

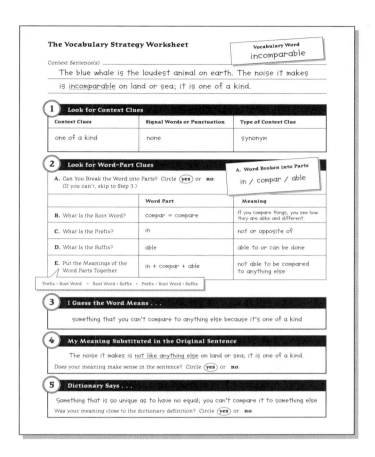

Guided Practice—Context and Word-Part Clues

Use interactive whiteboard technology to display The Vocabulary Strategy Worksheet. Say: *We are going to fill in this worksheet together. I will model on my worksheet, and you will copy what I write onto your worksheets. For the first example, we are going to figure out the meaning of the word* incomparable. On the worksheet, print *incomparable* in the box labeled Vocabulary Word and then copy the first two sentences of the excerpt—the context sentences. Have students do the same.

Point out to Spanish-speaking ELLs that *incomparable* and *incomparable* are identically spelled cognates.

> ▶ **1. Look for Context Clues**

Say: *Step 1 says to look for context clues in the words, phrases, and sentences surrounding* incomparable. Ask: *Can anyone find any context clues for* incomparable*?* (Possible answer: *one of a kind*) Say: *I am going to print the context clues in the box labeled Context Clues, and you should do the same.* Ask: *Do you see any*

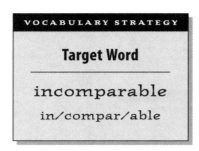

VOCABULARY STRATEGY

Target Word

incomparable

in/compar/able

152

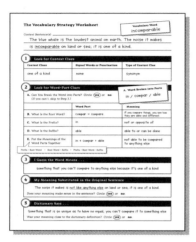

signal words or punctuation that might indicate the type of context clues we found? (no) *Let's print* none *in the box labeled Signal Words or Punctuation.* Now have students look at the Types of Helpful Context Clues chart. Ask: *What type of context clue did you find?* (synonym) Say: *Let's print* synonym *in the box labeled Type of Context Clue.*

▶ 2A. Look for Word-Part Clues—Can You Break the Word into Parts?

Have students look at Step 2A: Look for Word-Part Clues. Ask: *Can you break the word* incomparable *into parts?* (yes) Say: *Let's circle* yes *on the worksheet and break* incomparable *into three word parts—prefix, root word, and suffix—by drawing a slanted line between the parts. Let's print* in/compar/able *in the box labeled Word Broken into Parts.*

▶ 2B. Look for Word-Part Clues—What Is the Root Word?

Say: *Now we are going to look at each of the word parts in* incomparable. Ask: *What is the root word?* (compare) *That's right. On the worksheet, let's print* compare *in the box next to Root Word.* Ask: *Who knows what* compare *means?* (Possible answer: *If you compare things, you see how they are alike and how they are different.*) *Let's print the meaning on our worksheets.*

▶ 2C. Look for Word-Part Clues—What Is the Prefix?

Say: *Now let's look at the prefix.* Ask: *What is the prefix?* (in–) *On the worksheet, let's print* in– *next to Prefix.* Ask: *What is the meaning of the prefix* in–? (not or opposite of) Say: *That's right. Let's print the meaning on our worksheets.*

▶ 2D. Look for Word-Part Clues—What Is the Suffix?

Have students look at the suffix. Ask: *What is the suffix?* (–able) *On the worksheet, let's print* –able *next to Suffix.* Ask: *What is the meaning of the suffix* –able? (able to or can be done) Say: *That's right. Let's print the meaning on our worksheets.*

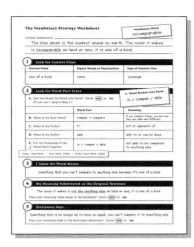

▶ **2E. Look for Word-Part Clues—
Put the Meanings of the Word Parts Together**

Say: *Now we're going to build the meaning of the whole word by putting the meanings of the three word parts together: prefix plus root word plus suffix.* Have students print the whole word *incomparable* on the worksheet. Ask: *Using the meanings of all of the word parts, what is the meaning of* incomparable? (not able to be compared to anything else) Say: *That's good. Let's print this meaning on our worksheets.*

▶ **3. I Guess the Word Means . . .**

Have students go to Step 3. Say: *In Step 3 we use both context clues and word-part clues to guess what the unfamiliar word means.* Ask: *In your own words, who can tell me what* incomparable *means?* (something so unusual it is not like anything else) Say: *That's a good guess. Let's print that meaning on our worksheets.*

▶ **4. My Meaning Substituted in the Original Sentence**

Direct students to Step 4. Say: *Now we are going to substitute our meaning in the original sentence.* Ask: *Who can say the sentence aloud, replacing* incomparable *with our meaning?* (The noise it makes is not like anything else on land or sea; it is one of a kind.) Say: *On our worksheets, let's print the original sentence, substituting our meaning for* incomparable. Ask: *Does the meaning we guessed make sense in the sentence?* (yes) *Let's circle* yes.

▶ **5. Dictionary Says . . .**

Direct students to Step 5. Ask: *Who wants to look up* incomparable *in the dictionary?* (The dictionary definition says that *incomparable* is "something that is so unique as to have no equal.") Ask: *Was our meaning close to the dictionary definition?* (yes) *Let's circle* yes *on the worksheet.*

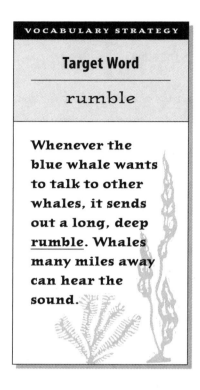

VOCABULARY STRATEGY

Target Word

rumble

Whenever the blue whale wants to talk to other whales, it sends out a long, deep rumble. Whales many miles away can hear the sound.

154

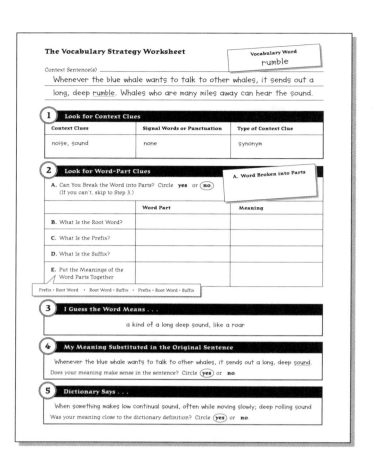

Guided Practice—Context Clues Only

Use interactive whiteboard technology to display The Vocabulary Strategy Worksheet. Say: *For the next example, we are going to focus on figuring out the meaning of the word* rumble. *I will model on my worksheet, and you will copy what I write onto your worksheets.* On the top of the worksheet, print the vocabulary word and the last two sentences of the excerpt. Have students do the same. Then ask a volunteer to read the sentences aloud. Tell students that sometimes they have to skip steps of The Vocabulary Strategy when there are no word-part clues to rely on.

▶ 1. Look for Context Clues

Ask: *Can anyone find any context clues for the word* rumble? (Possible answers: *noise, sound*) Say: *Let's print the context clues for* rumble *on our worksheets.* Ask: *Do you see any signal words*

or punctuation that might indicate the type of context clues we found? (no) *Let's print* none *in the box labeled Signal Words or Punctuation. Now let's look at the Types of Helpful Context Clues chart.* Ask: *What types of context clues did you find?* (synonym) Say: *Let's print* synonym *in the box labeled Type of Context Clue.*

▶ 2A. Look for Word-Part Clues—Can You Break the Word into Parts?

Say: *Now let's go to Step 2A. Can we break the word* rumble *into word parts?* (no) Say: *That's right, the word* rumble *is a single word that can't be broken into parts. Let's circle* no *and skip down to Step 3.*

▶ 3. I Guess the Word Means . . .

Say: *Step 3 tells us to use the context clues to guess what we think* rumble *means.* Ask: *In your own words, who can tell me what* rumble *means?* (a kind of long, deep sound, like a roar) Say: *That's a good guess. Let's print that meaning on our worksheets.*

▶ 4. My Meaning Substituted in the Original Sentence

Direct students to Step 4. Ask: *Who can read the sentence aloud, replacing* rumble *with our meaning?* (Whenever the blue whale wants to talk to other whales, it sends out a long, deep sound.) Say: *On our worksheets, let's print the original sentence, substituting our meaning for* rumble. Ask: *Does the meaning we guessed make sense in the sentence?* (yes) *Let's circle* yes.

▶ 5. Dictionary Says . . .

Have students go to Step 5. Ask: *Who wants to look up* rumble *in the dictionary to confirm our meaning?* (The dictionary says that rumble is "a low continual, or deep, rolling sound, often while moving slowly.") Ask: *Was our meaning close to the dictionary definition?* (yes) *Let's circle* yes *on our worksheets.*

156

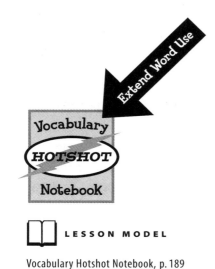

LESSON MODEL

Vocabulary Hotshot Notebook, p. 189

Independent Practice

Ask a volunteer to review the steps of The Vocabulary Strategy and how the strategy was used to figure out the meanings of *incomparable* and *rumble.* Select two words from a selection in students' social studies or science textbook. Print the words on the board. Then ask students to independently read the selection and apply The Vocabulary Strategy to figure out the words. Make sure students understand that they should use a separate worksheet for each targeted word. You may want to help students begin the assignment by going through the beginning steps with them.

When students have completed their worksheets, have them share their results as a group. Try to have them explain which strategy they found more useful, if they found the combination of both context clues and word-part clues more useful than either one alone, and if so, why.

CHAPTER

3

Word
Consciousness

what?
why?
when?
how?

Word Consciousness

> Students who are word conscious are aware of the words around them—those they read and hear and those they write and speak.
>
> —**GRAVES & WATTS-TAFFE, 2002**

Word Consciousness …

Awareness of words

Enjoyment of words

Playing with words

Interest in words

Appreciation of words

Satisfaction in using words well

ADEPT DICTION
the skillful use of words in speech and writing

Word consciousness can be defined simply as interest in and awareness of words (Anderson and Nagy 1992; Graves and Watts-Taffe 2002). According to Scott and Nagy (2004), "students need to become conscious of how words work and ways they can use them." Students who have developed word consciousness use words skillfully; they appreciate the subtleties of word meaning. More than that, word-conscious students are curious about language, like to play with words, and enjoy investigating the origins and histories of words.

Scott and Nagy (2004) believe that rather than treating it as an isolated component of vocabulary instruction "teachers need to take word consciousness into account throughout each and every day." One way to accomplish this is by building a classroom "rich with words" (Beck, McKeown, and Kucan 2002). A word-rich classroom environment is a place filled with all types of word resources, such as dictionaries, thesauruses, word walls, crossword puzzles, Scrabble and other word games, literature, poetry books, and word-play and joke books. It is a place that fosters the development of word consciousness.

Adept Diction

A word-rich environment supports the use of *adept diction*—"the skillful use of words in speech and writing" (Graves 2000). Teachers can model adept diction in their own choice of words, point out skillful use of words in the texts students are reading,

Fostering Word Consciousness

Adept Diction

- in teacher's use of language
- in reading texts
- in student's speech and writing
- beyond the classroom

Word Play

Word Histories and Origins

> The teacher who is alert to opportunities for using sophisticated, interesting, and precise language is probably the most important element in a word-rich environment.
>
> —BECK ET AL., 2002

and encourage students to expand the range of word choices in their own speech and writing (Graves 2000; Beck et al. 2002; Graves and Watts-Taffe 2002; Scott and Nagy 2004).

Teachers who deliberately use skillful language that intrigues and challenges students can set the tone for the classroom and motivate students to expand their verbal horizons and use more precise language. This type of modeling can become a natural part of the classroom conversation. For example, teachers can use the word *procrastinator* to describe a student who puts off doing assignments until the last minute, or say "please *refrain* from talking" to ask students to be quiet.

The texts students are reading offer another opportunity for recognizing skillful diction. Accomplished authors use precise and colorful words in their writing. In well-written literature, students can look for and collect "gifts of words," or phrases the author employed to paint a particularly vivid picture or to add texture or tone to the writing. Group discussion about these phrases (e.g., metaphors, similes, and descriptive language) provides an opportunity to talk about skillful choice of words, word meaning, and the author's use of language (Scott and Nagy 2004).

Precision in word choice plays a fundamental role in effective writing. Students should be encouraged to employ adept diction in their own writing. According to Scott and Nagy (2004), "In writing, unlike in conversation, word choice is one of the most important, if not the most important, tool for expressive power." Encouraging adroit word usage involves creating contexts in which students can experiment with new words (Graves and Watts-Taffe 2002). During writing conferences, a teacher might urge students to rethink word choices in an effort to make their writing more vivid, precise, or suitable for a particular audience (Graves 2000).

> Being a word-conscious teacher is the best way to promote word consciousness among students.
>
> —LANE & ALLEN, 2010

160

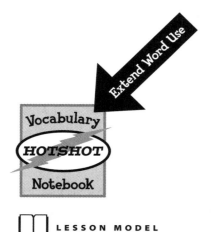

LESSON MODEL

Vocabulary Hotshot Notebook, p. 189

McKeown and Beck (2004) describe a successful vocabulary program as one in which "words do not appear as part of a classroom exercise and then drop from sight." They strongly suggest motivating students to take their vocabulary learning into the outside world: "The more students discover how words are used and where they appear outside the class, the greater the chance that they will really use the words in their own speaking and writing, and come to own them." Through nurturing this link between school and the outside world, vocabulary learning becomes less an isolated classroom-based activity.

To motivate students, teachers can reward them when they find—either hearing or seeing—the same words outside school that have been introduced as target words in school. For this purpose, Beck, Perfetti, and McKeown (1982) created a device they called a Word Wizard Chart. Teachers recorded target words on the chart and then challenged students to find these words in sources outside school, such as in books and newspapers, on the radio or television, on billboards, or in conversations. When students brought their sightings back to school, they earned points. The points were recorded next to each student's name on the chart in the classroom. Every few weeks, the teacher added up the points and gave students achievement awards.

Language Categories

Category	Word Origin	Definition	Examples
Synonyms	Greek, "same name"	Words that are very close in meaning	*happy/glad*
Antonyms	Greek, "opposite name"	Words that are opposite or nearly opposite in meaning	*up/down* *hot/cold*
Homographs	Greek, "same writing"	Words that are spelled the same but have different meanings and different origins	*bark* (tree covering) *bark* (sound a dog makes)

Language Categories

Synonyms

Antonyms

Homographs

DENOTATION
the literal meaning of
a word

CONNOTATION
the feeling associated
with a word

Alerting students to the ways that language is categorized contributes to adept diction. Being aware of relationships among words, such as synonyms, antonyms, and homographs, helps students to make finer distinctions in their word choices. *Synonyms* are words that are "very close in meaning." According to Templeton (1997), "When students study the fine gradations of meaning that separate synonyms, they learn progressively finer conceptual distinctions." These distinctions involve knowing both the denotations and connotations words can have. Denotation refers to the literal meaning of a word; for example, "not physically strong" is the denotative meaning of the word *weak.* Connotation refers to the feeling associated with a word. A word can have a positive, negative, or neutral connotation; for example, *weak* has a negative connotation when it means "lack of strength of character." Sometimes connotation is the difference in meaning between two synonyms.

Antonyms are words that are "opposite or nearly opposite in meaning." There are different types of antonym relationships. Polar, or complementary, antonyms have no middle ground. These antonym pairs either are mutually exclusive (e.g., girl and boy) or undo the meaning of each other (e.g., right and wrong). Scalar, or gradable, antonym pairs allow for gradations of meaning between them (e.g., happy and sad). Scalar antonyms can be useful for teaching analogies.

Homographs are "two or more words that are spelled the same but have different meanings and different origins." For example, *volume* ("how loud something is"), *volume* ("one book in a series of books"), and *volume* ("the amount of space that something occupies") are homographs. Homographs are often used in puns that play on the ambiguity of the words. For example, the pun "Time flies like a bird; fruit flies like melon" capitalizes on two different homograph pairs: *flies* (the verb) and *flies* (the insects), and *like* (the preposition) and *like* (the verb).

161

A good metaphor
implies an intuitive
perception of
the similarity of the
dissimilar.

—ARISTOTLE

162

 **LESSON MODELS**

Animal Idioms, p. 168

Five-Senses Simile Web, p. 183

Knowledge of terms such as antonym, synonym, and homograph is part of word consciousness, as is the ability to deal with figures of speech (Scott and Nagy 2004). Figurative language uses *figures of speech* that enable speakers and writers to express ideas in fresh, new ways. The most common figures of speech are similes, metaphors, and idioms. A simile is a comparison that is explicitly signaled by the word *like* or *as*. The term simile comes from the Latin root *similes,* meaning "like." Metaphors are comparisons that are not explicitly signaled by *like* or *as*. Coming from the Greek roots *meta,* meaning "over," and *phor,* meaning "carry," metaphors "carry over" a comparison or contrast with one object, event, or person to another object, event, or person. An idiom is a phrase or expression in which the entire meaning is different from the usual meanings of the individual words within it. Learning about idioms is useful in the vocabulary development of all students, but especially for ELLs, who often focus on the literal meanings of words. For example, "to cut the mustard," if taken literally, would not convey its true meaning: to do a capable job.

Figurative Language			
Figure of Speech	**Word Origin**	**Definition**	**Examples**
Simile	Latin, "like"	A comparison of two things that are not the same by using the word *like* or *as*	*as easy as pie* *float like a butterfly*
Metaphor	Greek, "carry over"	A comparison of two things that are not the same without using the word *like* or *as*	*My friend is a walking encyclopedia.*
Idiom		An expression that cannot be understood by the meanings of the individual words within it	*to cut the mustard* *to be in a pickle*

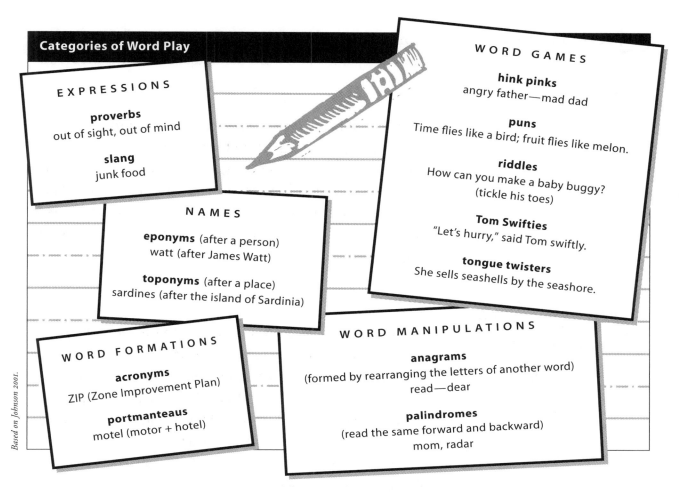

Categories of Word Play

EXPRESSIONS

proverbs
out of sight, out of mind

slang
junk food

NAMES

eponyms (after a person)
watt (after James Watt)

toponyms (after a place)
sardines (after the island of Sardinia)

WORD FORMATIONS

acronyms
ZIP (Zone Improvement Plan)

portmanteaus
motel (motor + hotel)

WORD GAMES

hink pinks
angry father—mad dad

puns
Time flies like a bird; fruit flies like melon.

riddles
How can you make a baby buggy?
(tickle his toes)

Tom Swifties
"Let's hurry," said Tom swiftly.

tongue twisters
She sells seashells by the seashore.

WORD MANIPULATIONS

anagrams
(formed by rearranging the letters of another word)
read—dear

palindromes
(read the same forward and backward)
mom, radar

Based on Johnson 2001.

163

Word play is sporting
with the medium
as medium....It plays
on sense and imagery
to create the humor
and nonsense of
unusual connections.

**—MOFFETT &
WAGNER, 1992**

Word Play

Research shows that word and language play can stimulate students' natural interest in and curiosity about language, help improve reading and vocabulary development, reveal the structures of language, and foster independent learning (Blachowicz and Fisher 2004; Johnson, Johnson, and Schlichting 2004; Graves 2000). Word play is "a playful attitude toward words in particular and language in general" (Graves 2000). It engages students in active, social learning, builds on children's natural curiosity about language, and provides the motivation to continue improving their language skills. Word play is accomplished through the manipulation of meanings, arrangements, sounds, spellings, and various other aspects of words (Johnson et al. 2004). Johnson (2001) organized types of word

164

play into categories such as names, expressions, word formations, word games, and word manipulations, as shown on the previous page.

Literature can be used to engage students in word play. Books in which plays on words are an important part of the story's humor lend themselves to raising word consciousness. Authors such as Dr. Seuss and Jack Prelutsky intentionally and strategically construct and play around with words so as to engage children in playful and humorous interactions with language (Johnson et al. 2004).

CONNECT TO THEORY

Try your hand at creating a Tom Swifty. A Tom Swifty is a type of word play named after Tom Swift, the fictional character featured in a series of adventure books published from 1910 to 1935. In book dialogue, Tom rarely said anything without a qualifying adverb; for example, "Tom said eagerly" or "Tom said jokingly." All Tom Swifties follow the same basic pattern: what Tom said and how Tom said it. In a true Tom Swifty, the adverb relates both properly and punningly to Tom's spoken words. Here are some examples:

"And that's another plus for you," said Tom positively.
"My pencil is dull," said Tom pointlessly.

Word Histories and Origins

Words, like living things, have histories that change over time. Knowing about the histories of words can help instill in students a greater consciousness and appreciation of them. Each word—along with its word parts—has a story behind it, which tells why the word has come to mean what it does. New words are coined to represent new ideas or objects: *internet, cyberspace, 'hood.* Old words can be applied to new situations:

Greek
Specialized words used mostly in science and technology.
astronaut, geology, automatic, barometer, phonograph, telephone

Latin
Longer, more sophisticated words used in formal contexts, such as content-area texts and literature.
audible, dictate, pedal, transport, inspect, construct

Anglo-Saxon
Short, everyday words used frequently in ordinary conversation and beginning reading texts.
house, happy, play, boy, girl

Layers of the English Language

bug, mouse, monitor, crash, drive. In addition, many words that were common in past years now have different or expanded meanings, or have become obsolete. *Bad* now means "good"; *cool* means "acceptable." *Gee whiz* and *jeepers* are hardly ever heard today.

Curiosity about words includes learning about their origins, too. The structure and origins of English words come primarily from Anglo-Saxon, Latin, and Greek (Henry 2003). The Anglo-Saxon layer is characterized by short, everyday words used frequently in ordinary conversation and beginning reading texts. The Latin layer consists of longer, more sophisticated words used in formal contexts such as content-area textbooks and literature. Latin is the basis for the Romance languages, including French, Italian, Portuguese, Romanian, and Spanish, all of which have contributed words to English. The Greek layer contains specialized words used mostly in science and technology. During the Renaissance, Greek words entered English by the thousands to meet the needs of scholars and scientists.

CONNECT

TO THEORY

Sorting words is one way to internalize what you have learned about the layers of the English language. Using the Layers of the English Language chart above and the chart of Common Greek and Latin Roots in English on p. 82, sort the following words according to their origin: Anglo-Saxon, Latin, or Greek. (See Answer Key, p. 198.)

WORD SORT: telephoto, table, respectful, predict, phonogram, pedestrian, micrometer, made, instructor, geocentric, export, branch, book, grapheme, audit, astrology, airplane, after, omit

why?

Word Consciousness

A huge step toward fostering word consciousness comes from simply recognizing that we want to make students consciously aware of words and their importance.

—GRAVES, 2000

Word consciousness forms the basis for a continuing love of words and language that students can carry with them beyond their school years (Anderson and Nagy 1992; Graves and Watts-Taffe 2002). According to Scott and Nagy (2004), one aspect of word consciousness, adept diction, is essential for sustained vocabulary growth. Skillful word choice enhances the ability to communicate ideas; it is essential to effective writing. Moreover, reflecting upon and paying attention to an author's choice of words contributes to reading comprehension. Word play, another aspect of word consciousness, helps students become more aware of the structure and rules of language. Understanding word play is a metacognitive act, or a conscious thought process. Word play also requires metalinguistic awareness, the ability to reflect on and manipulate units of language (Scott and Nagy 2004).

Providing an environment rich with words and word play can be especially helpful for word-deprived students. Blachowicz and Fisher (2002) found that students struggling with reading "almost universally" had not played word games either at home or at school, and that "When we invited them to do so, they often become animated and motivated learners."

Research Findings . . .

Word consciousness is crucial to learners' success in expanding the breadth and depth of students' word knowledge over the course of their lifetimes.

—GRAVES & WATTS-TAFFE, 2002

To effectively promote vocabulary growth, teachers must aim to help students develop vocabulary knowledge that is generative—*the kind of knowledge that will transfer to and enhance the acquisition of other words as well. Word consciousness is an aspect of generative vocabulary knowledge.*

—SCOTT & NAGY, 2004

Children learn best when they have strong personal interest and are actively and interactively involved with learning. . . . It is important that we incorporate word and language play activities in the classroom to stimulate, sustain, and recapture that natural interest.

—JOHNSON, JOHNSON & SCHLICHTING, 2004

Suggested Reading . . .

Bringing Words to Life: Robust Vocabulary Instruction, 2nd Edition (2013) by Isabel L. Beck, Margaret G. McKeown & Linda Kucan. New York: Guilford.

Teaching Vocabulary in All Classrooms, 5th Edition (2015) by Camille Blachowicz & Peter J. Fisher. New York: Pearson.

Teaching Word Meanings (2006) by Steven A. Stahl & William E. Nagy. London: Routledge.

The Vocabulary Book: Learning & Instruction, 2nd Edition (2016) by Michael F. Graves. New York: Teacher's College Press.

The Vocabulary Teacher's Book of Lists (2004) by Edward Bernard Fry. Hoboken, NJ: Wiley.

Vocabulary Instruction: Research to Practice, 2nd Edition (2012) Edited by Edward J. Kame'enui & James F. Baumann. New York: Guilford.

Word Consciousness

LESSON MODEL FOR

Word Consciousness

Benchmarks

- ability to interpret literal and figurative meanings of idioms
- ability to research origins of idioms

Grade Level

- Kindergarten and above

Grouping

- whole class
- small group or pairs

Materials

- small plastic toy horses
- drawing paper
- crayons or markers
- dictionaries

 **SEE ALSO . . .**

Reference Book

- *Scholastic Dictionary of Idioms* by Marvin Terban (New York: Scholastic, 1998)

Animal Idioms

An idiom is a phrase or expression in which the entire meaning is different from the usual meanings of the individual words within it. Idioms are fun to work with because they are part of everyday vocabulary. Students enjoy working with figurative meanings, as well as imagining possible literal meanings for the expressions. They also enjoy finding out about the origins of idiomatic expressions, some of which are very old. Introducing idioms by topic can make them easier for students to remember. This sample lesson model focuses on introducing idioms that make use of animals or animal comparisons.

Explanation

Tell students that an idiom is an expression that cannot be fully understood by the meanings of the individual words that are contained within it. The meaning of the whole idiom has little, often nothing, to do with the meanings of the words taken one by one. Point out to students that idioms are often used in writing or speech to make expression more colorful and that some of the most colorful English idioms make use of animals or animal comparisons. Explain that many idioms have interesting origins that may not make literal sense to us today, but made perfectly good sense during the times in which they were coined.

ANIMAL IDIOMS

Target Idioms

to hold your horses

to be raining cats and dogs

Learning about idioms can be particularly helpful for ELLs because the gap between the literal meaning of individual words and the intended meaning of the expression often causes trouble in translation.

Tell students that the expression "to hold your horses" is an idiom. Demonstrate its literal meaning by holding a bunch of small plastic toy horses in your hand. Tell students that when someone tells you "to hold your horses" it would be silly to think that they wanted you to hold a bunch of horses in your hand. The whole expression "to hold your horses" actually means "to slow down, wait a minute, or be more patient." For example, if you were impatiently waiting for your sister to get off the phone, your sister might say to you, "Hold your horses. I'll be off the phone in a minute!"

Tell students that "to be raining cats and dogs" is another idiom. Ask students whether, if someone said it's "raining cats and dogs," they would expect to look up and see animals falling from the sky. Then explain to them that "raining cats and dogs" is used to describe when it's raining really heavily or really hard. Ask volunteers to describe a time they remember when it was "raining cats and dogs."

Ask students to draw pictures of the literal meaning of either "to hold your horses" or "to be raining cats and dogs." Then have them take turns showing their illustration and using the idiom correctly in a context sentence.

ANIMAL IDIOMS

Target Idiom

to let the cat out
of the bag

Animal Idioms

- to have ants in your pants
- to take the bull by the horns
- to let the cat out of the bag
- to have the cat get your tongue
- to be raining cats and dogs
- the straw that broke the camel's back
- to have a cow
- to wait until the cows come home
- to be in the doghouse
- to let sleeping dogs lie
- to be in a fine kettle of fish
- to seem a little fishy
- to live high on the hog
- to look a gift horse in the mouth
- to eat like a horse
- to hear it straight from the horse's mouth
- to hold your horses
- to put the cart before the horse
- to change horses in midstream
- to be a wolf in sheep's clothing

Collaborative Practice

Tell students that they are going to work together in groups to make a drawing of an animal idiom's literal meaning and then act out its real, or figurative, meaning. They will see if the drawings and skits they make provide enough information for their classmates to figure out what the idiom really means. To begin, select a group of three students to demonstrate the activity. Tell this group that their idiom is "to let the cat out of the bag" and that this idiom means "to give away a secret."

Divide the group tasks as follows: One student will draw the idiom the way it would look if it meant literally what it said: by drawing a sketch of a cat leaping out of a paper bag. This student labels the drawing with the idiom, "to let the cat out of the bag." The other two students develop a brief skit about the figurative meaning of the idiom: "to give away a secret." For example, they could develop a simple scene where someone finds out about a surprise birthday party, because a brother or sister gives it away beforehand. The last line could be: "You let the cat out of the bag."

When the group is finished, have them show the idiom's literal meaning in the drawing, and then act out its figurative meaning in the skit. Have the group challenge their classmates to guess the idiom's figurative, or intended, meaning and then correctly use the idiom in a sentence: *Nancy let the cat out of the bag when she told Nick about the surprise birthday party.*

When the whole class has understood how this activity works, assign a different animal idiom, with its figurative meaning, to other groups of students. Each group then works out its plan for making the drawing and acting out the skit. Have the groups take turns demonstrating their idioms to the class, so the class can guess the idiom's figurative meaning and use it in a sentence.

Other Idioms
• to be in a pickle
• to beat around the bush
• to bite off more than you can chew
• to burn your bridges
• to catch someone red-handed
• to cost an arm and a leg
• to cut corners
• to get up on the wrong side of the bed
• to have a chip on your shoulder
• to have something up your sleeve
• to know the ropes
• to make ends meet
• to pay through the nose
• to pull strings
• to see eye to eye
• to shoot the breeze
• to spill the beans
• to stick your neck out
• to take a rain check
• to touch something with a ten-foot pole
• to turn over a new leaf
• to wear your heart on your sleeve

Extend Word Knowledge

Students in intermediate grades will enjoy extending the idiom activity outlined above by searching out idiom origins. For example, "to hold your horses" is from the 1800s in America, a time before automobiles. If a carriage driver was letting his team of horses go too fast, he was told to "hold his horses." By pulling back on the horses' reins, the driver could slow the horses to a stop. It is believed that "raining cats and dogs" may have come from Norse mythology in which dogs were associated with windy storms and cats were associated with rain. Today the idiom "to let the cat out of the bag" has nothing to do with a cat or a bag, but hundreds of years ago it actually did. When buying a pig at a farmers' market, a favorite trick of a dishonest merchant was to put a worthless cat into your bag instead of a costly pig. You might not find out about the trick until you got home and let the cat out of the bag.

To research the origin of a particular idiom, students can use a book like the *Scholastic Dictionary of Idioms,* if it is available. If not, have them make use of online resources for idioms, which are many and varied. Show them how to Google the idiom, in quotes, and add the word origins after it to find numerous references. After completing the research, a group can share their idiom's literal and figurative meaning with the class. Then the group can develop and sketch and act out the idiom's original meaning, challenging the class to explain the origin of the idiom, as well as how the idiom's original meaning relates to its currently used figurative meaning.

LESSON MODEL FOR

Word Consciousness

Benchmark

• ability to understand Latin and Greek number prefixes

Grade Level

• Grade 4 and above

Grouping

• whole class
• small group or pairs
• individual

Materials

• dictionaries

Latin and Greek Number Words

Latin and Greek number morphemes are often called prefixes because they appear at the beginning of words (Henry 2003). Teaching Latin- and Greek-based number words is useful because these words appear over and over in upper-grade math and science textbooks. This sample lesson model focuses on becoming aware of and then playing with number prefixes and number words.

● ●

Explanation

Remind students that a prefix is a word part added to the beginning of a root word that changes its meaning. Tell students that many English words begin with number prefixes from Latin or Greek. It is important to know these prefixes because related number words appear over and over, especially in math and science textbooks. Explain that in this lesson they are going to have a little bit of fun with number prefixes.

Explain that Latin number prefixes are found at the beginning of words in categories such as groups of musicians (*tet* as in *quartet*), multiples of something (*uple* as in *quadruple*), number of sides of something (*lateral* as in *quadrilateral*), number of years between two events (*ennial* as in *quadrennial*), and words for large numbers (*illion* as in *quadrillion*). Then point out that Greek number prefixes are found at the beginning of words in categories such as the number of sides of plane figures (*gon* as in *pentagon*), number of faces of solid figures (*hedron* as in *pentahedron*), number of angles (*angle* as in *pentangle*), and number of events in an athletic competition (*athlon* as in *pentathlon*).

Display a Number Prefixes chart, such as the one shown on the facing page. Go over the Latin and Greek prefixes for each numeral and the related words they can form. Make sure to explain to students the meaning of each of the related words.

Number Prefixes			
Numeral	**Latin**	**Greek**	**Related Words**
1	uni–	mono–	unicycle, monotone
2	bi–, duo–	di–	bilingual, duet, dichotomy
3	tri–	tri–	triangle, trilateral, triple
4	quad–	tetra–	quadruple, tetrahedron
5	quint–	penta–	quintuplet, pentagon
6	sex–	hex–	sextuplet, hexagon
7	sept–	hept–	septet, heptagon
8	octa–	octo–	octagonal, octopus
9	non–, nove–	ennea–	nonagon, novena, ennead
10	deci–	dec–, deca–	decimal, decade, decathlon
100	cent–	hect–	centennial, hectogram
1,000	milli–	kilo–	millipede, kilobyte
10,000		myria–	myriad
1,000,000		mega–	megabyte, megawatt
1,000,000,000		giga–	gigabyte, gigahertz

> unicycle
> bicycle
> tricycle

Guided Practice

Now print the words *unicycle*, *bicycle*, and *tricycle* on the board. Ask students to use the Number Prefixes chart to answer the following questions:

• How many wheels does a unicycle have? (*one*) What is the number prefix? (*uni–*) Draw one wheel next to the word *unicycle*.

• How many wheels does a bicycle have? (*two*) What is the number prefix? (*bi–*) Draw two wheels next to the word *bicycle*.

• How many wheels does a tricycle have? (*three*) What is the number prefix? (*tri–*) Draw three wheels next to the word *tricycle*.

Latin Number Words
athletic events: biathlon, triathlon, tetrathlon, pentathlon, heptathlon, decathlon
groups of musicians: duet, trio, quartet, quintet, sextet, septet, octet, nonet, dectet
multiples: triple, quadruple, quintuple, sextuple, septuple, octuple, nonuple, decuple

Greek Number Words
sides of plane figures: triangle, tetragon, pentagon, hexagon, heptagon, octagon, enneagon, nonagon, decagon
years between events: biennial, triennial, quadrennial, quinquennial, centennial

Now ask students to use the Number Prefixes chart to answer the following category-related questions:

- If eight people sing in an octet, how many people sing in a quartet? (*four*) In a septet? (*seven*)

- If three countries make a trilateral agreement, how many countries would be involved in a bilateral agreement? (*two*)

- If a triangle has three angles, how many angles in a quadrangle? (*four*)

- If a pentagon has five sides, how many sides in an octagon? (*eight*) In a hexagon? (*six*)

- If a decathlon has ten athletic events, how many events are there in a triathlon? (*three*) In a biathlon? (*two*)

- If a centennial is the one-hundredth-year anniversary, what is a bicentennial? (*a two-hundredth-year anniversary*)

- If a megawatt is a million watts of electricity, what is a kilowatt? (*one thousand watts*)

Collaborative Practice

QUESTION MASTER GAME Prepare students by telling them that today they will get to be the "question master"—the person who makes up questions and asks others to find the answers. The question master uses the Number Prefixes chart to make up questions for the rest of the class to answer. Then the rest of the class tries to answer the questions. For example, the question master might ask:

- If two computers are for sale at the same price—one with 50 megabytes of memory, and one with 50 gigabytes—which one would you buy? (*50 gigabytes*) Why? (*You get more for the same price.*)

- How many kilobytes are in a gigabyte? (*one million*)

- Would it be faster to count the legs on a bug called a milli-pede or on a bug called a centipede? (*a centipede*) Why? (*fewer number of legs*)

Allow as many students as possible to play the role of question master. Students will probably need time to prepare questions. To facilitate the process, you might want to have students work in groups of two or three.

Number Prefix Riddles

NUMBER PREFIX RIDDLES   Students can also use number prefixes to create riddles. In this case, the answers to the riddles are made-up words that contain number prefixes. The made-up words are usually plays on real words. To begin, have students work in pairs or groups of three. Tell them that each group is to try to make up one or more riddles using made-up words they create with number prefixes. They then ask the class to answer them. To conclude, they will put the best riddles together to make a class book of number riddles.

To give students the idea, write two or more of these examples on the board:

- What do you call a four-armed octopus? (*a quadropus*)

- What would you call a cycle that had one million wheels? (*a megacycle*)

- An announcer said, "Barry Bonds just hit another quadruple." What is the usual baseball name for a quadruple? (*a home run*)

When students have made up their own riddles, have them present the riddles to the class to figure out. The class can vote on the most original, funniest, and hardest riddle. They can also decide on which riddles can go in the number riddle book.

LESSON MODEL FOR

Word Consciousness

Benchmarks

- ability to identify complementary and gradable antonym pairs
- ability to scale antonyms

Grade Level

- Grade 4 and above

Prerequisite

- knowing about antonyms

Grouping

- whole class
- small group or pairs

Materials

- dictionaries and thesauruses

Antonym Scales

Opposites, or antonyms, are among the first word relationships children learn; for example, soon after children learn the meaning of *up,* they learn the meaning of *down.* In this sample lesson model, students are introduced to two kinds of antonyms: complementary and gradable. Once they see the difference between the two types, students focus on gradable antonyms, learning how to arrange words in a scale, or semantic gradient. Antonym scales help students to see and express the degrees of meaning between gradable antonym pairs. They also serve to enhance students' adept diction, or skillful use of words.

Explanation

Remind students that antonyms are words that are "opposite or nearly opposite in meaning." For example, the opposite of *top* is *bottom*; the opposite of *hot* is *cold*; the opposite of *yes* is *no.* Then tell students that there are two types of antonyms. The first type is called *complementary.* These are words, like *up* and *down,* that express an either/or relationship. An elevator is either going *up* or *down*; there's no in-between movement. Then explain that the second type is called *gradable.* These are antonyms, like *hot* and *cold,* that form opposite ends of a continual scale. Point out that we can name many other temperatures between hot and cold, such as *cool* or *warm.* To illustrate both types, print these examples on the board:

> Complementary Antonyms: push/pull, dead/alive, off/on, sink/float, right/wrong, absent/present
>
> Gradable Antonyms: ugly/beautiful, best/worst, dark/light, fast/slow, good/bad, hot/cold

ANTONYMS

boy / girl
wet / dry
true / false
happy / sad

Guided Practice

Print several antonym pairs on the board and have the class decide whether each pair is complementary or gradable. For example: *boy/girl, true/false* (complementary); *wet/dry, happy/sad* (gradable). Students may need help in thinking some of these through.

Now invite students to think of other complementary antonym pairs to add to those they have identified above. Remind them that in complementary pairs, if one exists, the other cannot. You can also point out that, usually, thinking of one automatically brings up the other. If students have trouble, you can help by naming the first element in the following pairs—*send/receive, give/take, married/single, sink/float, remember/forget*—and having them say the other.

ANTONYM SCALE

excellent A
good   B
fair   C
poor   D

Explain to students that they are going to use gradable antonyms to make an antonym scale. Tell them they are familiar with this type of scale from school: grades given for schoolwork form a scale, from A to D—from excellent at best to poor at worst—or whatever your grading scale happens to be. To illustrate this point, on the board draw an antonym scale like the one shown at left. Discuss the scale. Then ask students where they think terms such as *terrific, fantastic,* and *okay* would go on the scale. (Answers may vary.) Point out that gradable antonyms all have in-between terms that can be placed on a scale like this.

ANTONYM SCALE

red-hot
boiling
hot
warm
cool
cold
freezing
subzero

ANTONYM SCALE

magnificent
gorgeous
beautiful
attractive
plain
ugly
repulsive
hideous

Collaborative Practice

Now tell students that they are going to work in pairs to make their own antonym scale. The scale is about temperature and it goes from *red-hot* to *subzero*. Then print the following words on the board in random order: *boiling, warm, hot, cool, red-hot, cold, subzero, freezing.*

Ask the class to tell you which is the word for the absolute hottest. (*red-hot*) Which is the word for the absolute coldest? (*subzero*) Then go through the list with them, finding the next hottest (*boiling*) and so on, placing the words in order according to their degree of hot or cold in the temperature scale. The order from top to bottom should be: *red-hot, boiling, hot, warm, cool, cold, freezing, subzero.*

When the temperature scale is completed, tell students that you have another scale for them to do on their own. This scale is about appearance and it goes from *hideous* to *magnificent*. Print the following words on the board in random order: *hideous, gorgeous, ugly, attractive, beautiful, plain, magnificent, repulsive.*

Tell students they are to arrange the words in order from *hideous* to *magnificent*. Have students work in pairs to make their scale. Point out that they can consult a dictionary or a thesaurus to help them arrange the words. When they have completed their scales, have students present their ordered scale and say why they chose *beautiful* over *attractive* or *magnificent* over *gorgeous*. The order from top to bottom could be: *magnificent, gorgeous, beautiful, attractive, plain, ugly, repulsive, hideous.* Ask if there are other terms to describe appearance that would fit on this scale.

GRADABLE ANTONYMS

dark/light
big/small
early/late
easy/difficult
fancy/plain
fast/slow
rich/poor

Independent Practice

Print the following gradable antonym pairs on the board: *dark/light, big/small, early/late, easy/difficult, fancy/plain, fast/slow, rich/poor.* Have pairs of students pick a gradable antonym pair from the list and make a scale on their own. If they prefer, they can select their own gradable antonym pair. Tell the pairs to arrange the words from one extreme to the other to show degrees of meaning. Remind them that they do not necessarily have to start with either of the words they've chosen—there may be more extreme words for both ends. For example, *hot/cold* only describes the scale; *red-hot* and *boiling* are both more extreme than *hot.* Remind them also that different people start in different ways. Though most begin with the most extreme pair and fill in the middle terms, others begin in the middle with *warm* and work to both extremes, *boiling* and *subzero.*

When pairs have completed their scales, have them present the scales to the rest of the class. Ask pairs to justify the order they chose and also describe how they went about their task: choosing the most extreme ends first and filling in the middle, or starting in the middle and moving to the extremes, or some other way.

Extend Word Knowledge

Some verbally adept students might also enjoy deciding which is the most appropriate antonym for any given word. For example, given the words *tall, little, big, short, small,* and *large,* students might enjoy discussing why they think the best choices are *tall/short, big/little,* and *large/small,* but not *large/little* or *big/short.* Similarly, why does *good/terrible* not express antonym opposition as well as *good/bad* or *excellent/terrible*? Other difficulties might arise with what are called "near opposites," like *giant/dwarf, shout/whisper, town/country,* and *work/play.*

179

LESSON MODEL FOR

Word Consciousness

Benchmarks

- ability to use modern homographs
- ability to understand that word meanings evolve and change over time

Grade Level

- Grade 3 and above

Prerequisite

- knowing about homographs

Grouping

- whole class
- small group or pairs
- individual

Materials

- dictionaries

Web Word Web

Semantic webs, or word webs, make word meanings and word relationships visible. By putting word meanings into graphic form, word webs display the variety of meanings a word can have, and show the semantic relatedness of target words to other words and concepts.

In English, the oldest, most common words seem to have developed varied meanings over time. These words with identical spelling but a variety of meanings are called homographs. Word webs can help students—especially English-language learners—in sorting out these varied and changing meanings of common words. The sample lesson model utilizes a word web for focusing students' attention on modern uses for the word *web*, as in the World Wide Web.

Explanation

Tell students that language changes over time. New words are created to represent new ideas and new inventions. In the case of computer terminology, many old words have been given new meanings. One example is the word *mouse*. Until recently, the word *mouse* commonly meant "a small furry rodent with a long tail," but now the word *mouse* also describes "a small handheld device that plugs into a computer."

Remind students that they have previously learned about homographs and that homographs are words that are spelled the same but have different meanings and different origins. Point out that *mouse* the animal and *mouse* the computer device are homographs. Ask students to make quick pencil sketches illustrating the two meanings for *mouse*. After comparing their sketches, ask students if they can guess how the computer mouse got its name. (Possible response: *They have similar shapes and the cord looks like a long tail.*)

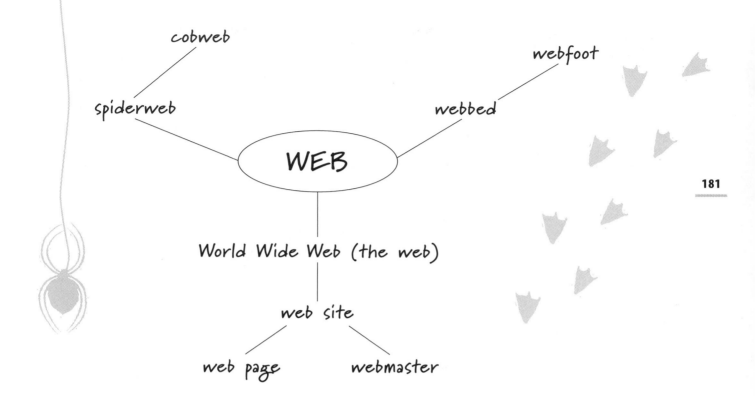

WORD WEB

Target Word
——————————
web

Guided Practice

Tell students that another common word that has a new high-tech meaning is *web*. Explain to students that they are going to help you to make a word web and that a word web is a drawing that shows how words can be related in meaning. To begin, print the word *web* in the center of the board. Have students brainstorm the various meanings for the word *web*. For each new meaning draw a connecting line from the center to the printed meaning. From each new meaning draw further lines to related words extending from the new word. This creates a word web with multiple connections for the word *web,* as shown above.

When the word web is completed, point out to students that it shows not only the older meanings of *web,* but also its newer meanings. Take the time to discuss each meaning and its connections. For example, from the meaning of *web* as a "delicate woven structure" comes *spiderweb* with all its connecting threads, which is related to *cobweb,* a spiderweb covered with

Computer Term Homographs

- application
- bug
- chat
- chip
- crash
- disk
- hard drive
- memory
- monitor
- mouse
- net
- program
- ram
- surf
- web

dust. For *webbed,* "a membrane of skin joining the digits of an animal's foot," name animals with webbed feet, such as ducks. Point out that the *World Wide Web* is often just called the *Web.* The World Wide Web is part of the Internet, a complex network. From the *World Wide Web* comes the related term *website,* "a group of related pages on the web," and from *website,* the related terms *web page,* "one page of information on a website," and *webmaster,* "a person responsible for the creation or maintenance of a website." Have students discuss the meanings and relationships of all these words. Then invite students to suggest other words to add to the word web, such as *web browser, webcam,* or *webcast.* Discuss the meaning and placement of each of the words.

Finally, you may wish to ask students if they can imagine why the World Wide Web is called a *web* in the first place. (Possible response: *It's a virtual space where you make connections to other people and places; from those connections arise still further connections, as in a spider's web or a fishnet or the word web they are creating.*)

Extend Word Knowledge

To extend the web activity, have students brainstorm a list of other computer terms that are homographs; for example, *application, bug, chat, chip, crash, disk, hard drive, memory, monitor, net, program, ram,* or *surf.* Then have pairs of students choose one term and make their own word webs. Tell them they may consult a dictionary to find more meanings for their target word.

When they have completed their webs, students can share their work with the rest of the class and discuss the connections they have discovered. Allow others in the class to help by adding connections that may have been missed. You may wish to display the webs on a classroom bulletin board.

LESSON MODEL FOR

Word Consciousness

Benchmarks

• ability to use adept diction
• ability to write similes

Grade Level

• Grade 2 and above

Prerequisite

• knowing about similes and synonyms

Grouping

• whole class

Activity Master

• Five-Senses Simile Web (Resources)

Materials

• PDF and copies of Five-Senses Simile Web
• chart paper

Five-Senses Simile Web

Engaging all the senses helps students in the production of many types of figurative language, especially similes. The Five-Senses Simile Web, based on the research of Graves and Watts-Taffe (2002), does this in a graphic way. Using words they have read or otherwise encountered, students construct simile webs by drawing lines from the target word to descriptions on how the word relates to each of the five senses. They try to describe how an abstract word smells, tastes, looks, sounds, and feels. This sample lesson model gives students a new and enjoyable way to engage with words as they learn about the sensory comparisons used widely in similes.

Explanation

Remind students that a simile is a comparison of two unlike things using the word *as* or *like*. Tell students that they are going to use the five senses to create a simile web for *boredom.* Begin by asking volunteers to explain what they think *boredom* means. Accept any reasonable answers, such as "If you are bored, you feel tired and impatient because you are not interested in something or because you have nothing to do."

Guided Practice

Use interactive whiteboard technology to display the Five-Senses Smile Web. Print the word *boredom* in the center. Now ask students to link *boredom* to specific sensory images. Ask them to imagine what the word *boredom* smells like, tastes like, feels like, sounds like, and looks like. Use their responses to fill in the simile web. The web should look something like the one on the following page, with sample responses shown.

Target Word

boredom

FIVE-SENSES SIMILE WEB

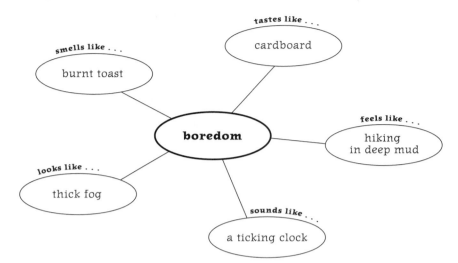

Boredom

Boredom smells like . . .
Burnt toast
Water

Boredom tastes like . . .
Cardboard
Dry grass

Boredom looks like . . .
Thick fog
A rainy day

Boredom sounds like . . .
A ticking clock
Silence

Boredom feels like . . .
Hiking in deep mud
Being alone

Now have students elaborate on their ideas by revising their suggested similes, encouraging thoughtful, unusual, or offbeat suggestions. That is, on the simile web replace some of the image words with synonyms. For example, *hiking* under "feels like" could be changed to *slogging*. *Thick fog* under "looks like" could be changed to *soupy fog*. Emphasize that the more vivid and precise their sense images are, the better the picture is that students create for themselves and for their readers.

Collaborative Practice

Tell students that poets use sensory images regularly. Have the class dictate a collaborative poem about boredom, with each student contributing a simile for each of the five senses. Write the collaborative poem on chart paper and have students take turns reading it aloud.

Written Practice

Students in intermediate grades can be asked to make their own simile webs for more complex words. For example, a web can be constructed for the word *anticipation*. Begin by asking for volunteers to explain what they think *anticipation* means. Accept any reasonable answers, such as "If you anticipate something pleasant or exciting that is going to happen, you look forward to it with pleasure."

FIVE-SENSES SIMILE WEB

Target Word

anticipation

Give each student a copy of the Five-Senses Simile Web. Then use the interactive whiteboard technology to display the web. Print the word *anticipation* in the center of the web and have students do the same. Now ask students to imagine what the word *anticipation* smells like, tastes like, feels like, sounds like, and looks like. As a group, fill in the first sense, "smells like." Then have students complete the web on their own, finding a sensory association for each of the remaining senses. Point out to students that they can make their sensory similes more colorful by carefully choosing the most precise words.

FIVE-SENSES SIMILE WEB

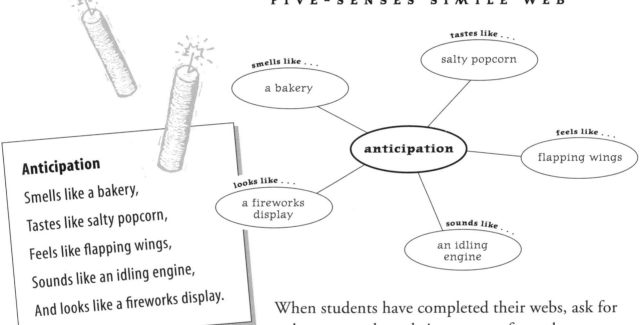

Anticipation

Smells like a bakery,

Tastes like salty popcorn,

Feels like flapping wings,

Sounds like an idling engine,

And looks like a fireworks display.

When students have completed their webs, ask for volunteers to share their responses for each sensory mode. Make sure all students understand that they are seeking to expand their understanding of the word *anticipation* by imagining how it would be interpreted by each of their senses.

Then ask students to use their *anticipation* simile webs to write poems. When they have finished, students can read their poems aloud to the class. Discuss with them how using the senses helps to enlarge the idea of what a word means, and how its meaning can best be conveyed to others.

LESSON MODEL FOR
Word Consciousness

Benchmarks

- ability to use adept diction in writing
- ability to use synonyms and antonyms
- ability to write diamante and cinquain poems

Grade Level

- Grade 3 and above

Prerequisite

- knowing about antonyms, synonyms, and syllables

Grouping

- whole class
- small group or pairs

Materials

- dictionaries

Poetry as Word Play

Writing poetry is well suited for word play. Poets are, after all, writers whose use of words is both skillful and playful. Students can also play with words and find that they wind up with poems. One effective way to introduce students to this type of word play is to engage them in writing poetry. This sample lesson model focuses on two poetic forms: diamantes and cinquains. A diamante is a diamond-shaped poem with seven lines. It can be used to explore either antonyms or synonyms. A cinquain has five lines, with each line having a specific number of syllables.

Diamante Poems

Tell students that a diamante is a seven-line poem in the shape of a diamond. In a diamante, each line uses specific kinds of words, such as adjectives or *–ing* words. Explain that diamantes are created using either antonym pairs or synonym pairs. On a handout, provide an example of an antonym diamante poem and information about its structural form, as shown below and on the facing page.

ANTONYM DIAMANTE Read the antonym diamante poem aloud. Then explain the form of a diamante to students by comparing this diamante with the chart showing its structural form. Explain that the words in the first and last lines are antonyms, and then point out the different parts of speech in each line. Discuss Line 4, the middle of the poem, and explain how it provides a transition between the antonyms in Lines 1 and 7.

Asleep
Comfy, cozy
Slumbering, snuggling, dreaming
Night, rest, dawn, shine
Blinking, yawning, stretching
Alive, alert
Awake

Antonym Diamante Poem

STRUCTURAL FORM OF AN ANTONYM DIAMANTE POEM

LINE 1:	Antonym 1
LINE 2:	Two adjectives describing Antonym 1
LINE 3:	Three *–ing* words describing Antonym 1
LINE 4:	Two nouns related to Antonym 1; two nouns related to Antonym 2
LINE 5:	Three *–ing* words describing Antonym 2
LINE 6:	Two adjectives describing Antonym 2
LINE 7:	Antonym 2

187

Now ask students to write their own antonym diamante poems. First have them brainstorm a list of antonym pairs, such as *asleep* and *awake*. Write the list on the board and ask students to choose an antonym pair to use in the development of their poem. Tell students to begin by filling in Line 1 with one of the antonyms in the pair (Antonym 1) and Line 7 with the other antonym in the pair (Antonym 2). Encourage students to consult a dictionary or thesaurus for help in selecting words. When students have finished writing, encourage them to share their antonym diamante poems with the class.

SYNONYM DIAMANTE Now challenge students to write their own synonym diamante poems. Explain that a synonym diamante follows the same structural form as an antonym diamante, except that Lines 1 and 7 are synonyms and in Line 4 the four nouns relate to both Synonym 1 and Synonym 2.

Synonym Diamante Poem

Ocean
Endless, blue
Sparkling, shifting, drifting
Whitecaps, swells, tides, waves
Rising, splashing, crashing
Powerful, ceaseless
Sea

STRUCTURAL FORM OF A CINQUAIN POEM

LINE 1:	Two syllables—a one-word subject, a noun
LINE 2:	Four syllables—two adjectives describing the subject
LINE 3:	Six syllables—three *-ing* words describing the subject
LINE 4:	Eight syllables—a descriptive phrase about the subject
LINE 5:	Two syllables—a synonym for the subject, a noun

Cinquain Poems

Baby Duck

Duckling

Yellow, downy

Waddling, dunking, splashing

A baby bird in the water

Quacker

Football

Lineman

Bull-necked, slammer

Rising, charging, tackling

Sunday nightmare of quarterbacks

Trencher

Cinquain Poems

Tell students that a cinquain is a five-line poem describing a person, place, or thing. Point out that the word *cinq* means "five" in French and that the five lines of a cinquain have two, four, six, eight, and two syllables, respectively. In addition, most lines have a specific number of words.

On a handout, provide examples of a cinquain poem and information about its structural form, as shown on this page. Read the cinquain poems aloud. Then count their lines and the number of syllables in each line. Explain the form of a cinquain poem to students by comparing it with the chart showing its structural form.

Now have students choose topics and write cinquains of their own. To help them in this exercise, you may wish to have students work in pairs or groups of three. Make clear that they may have to experiment with several word choices before finding those that fit. This is part of the "play" of poetry. Some students may have trouble limiting the syllables. If so, have them write cinquains following the internal structure only, focusing on word choice and descriptive requirements rather than the exact syllabication for each line.

LESSON MODEL FOR
Word Consciousness

Benchmarks

- ability to keep track of target vocabulary words
- ability to extend word use beyond the classroom

Grade Level

- Grade 2 and above

Grouping

- whole class
- small group or pairs
- individual

Sample Text

- "Alaska Adventure" (Resources)

Activity Master

- Vocabulary Hotshot Notebook Page (Resources)

Materials

- PDF and copies of Vocabulary Hotshot Notebook Page
- three-ring binders
- three-hole punched paper
- Vocabulary Hotshot Scoreboard
- dictionaries

Vocabulary Hotshot Notebook

Developing an in-depth and permanent understanding of new vocabulary comes through frequent encounters and use. Research makes clear that students do not own the new words they learn after only one exposure. Rather, it takes repeated reinforcement with a new word for a student to be able to use it confidently in speech or writing (Beck et al. 2002).

One way to ensure ongoing vocabulary learning is for students to keep a personal vocabulary notebook (McKeown and Beck 2004). Another way is by using devices such as a Word Wizard Chart (Beck et al. 1982). The Vocabulary Hotshot Notebook combines these two methods. Designed to motivate student interest in words, it provides a place and an opportunity for students not only to record target words, but also to keep track of these new words as they encounter them in the outside world. It is also a motivational activity in which students earn points for seeing, hearing, or using the target words in places outside the classroom. This sample lesson model can be adapted and used to enhance vocabulary instruction in any commercial reading program.

● ●

How to Make a Vocabulary Hotshot Notebook

1. Using three-hole punched paper and two-sided copying, make eight copies of the Vocabulary Hotshot Notebook Page per student (i.e., four sheets of paper, for 16 words).

2. Put the pages into a three-ring binder for each student.

CONTINUED ▷

189

190

Explanation

Distribute the Vocabulary Hotshot Notebooks to students. Explain to students that they will use their Vocabulary Hotshot Notebooks to keep track of new vocabulary words introduced in class and to make the new words their own. After entering the new vocabulary words in their notebooks, students will be on the lookout for the words in places and sources both inside and outside school: in other books, on signs, on bulletin boards, in newspapers and magazines, on the radio or on television, on billboards, or in conversations. Tell students that they will earn points for recording these encounters in their notebooks, and that the encounters can be with the word itself or a word in the same family. The goal is to earn enough notebook points in two weeks to become a Vocabulary Hotshot.

LEVELS OF ACHIEVEMENT   Prepare a Vocabulary Hotshot Scoreboard, such as the one shown below. Referring to the scoreboard, explain the levels of achievement to students. Tell them that there are three categories of winners: Hotshots, Big Shots, and Little Shots. They must earn 40 points to be a Hotshot, 30 points to be a Big Shot, and 20 points to be a Little Shot. At the end of two weeks, students' names will be recorded on the scoreboard according to the number of notebook points they earned.

Vocabulary HOTSHOT Scoreboard	Hotshots 40 points	Big Shots 30 points	Little Shots 20 points
	Billy	Anna	Jimmy
	Linda	Jamal	Barbara
	Marco	Ricardo	Matt
	Kenesha	Patricia	Sandy
	Isabel	Lin Yeng	Simon

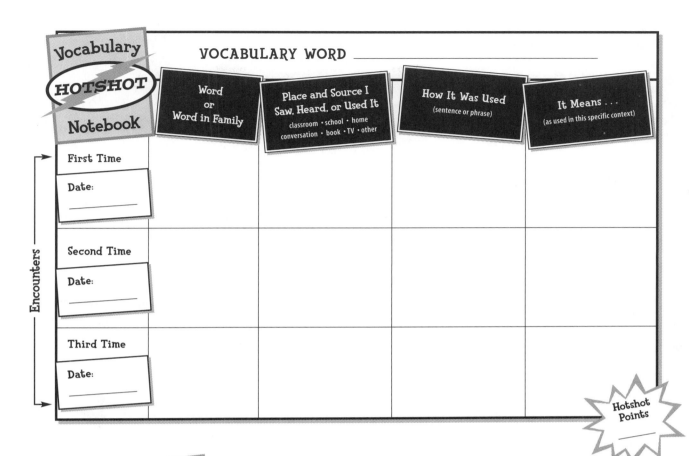

Vocabulary HOTSHOT Notebook

VOCABULARY WORD _____

Encounters		Word or Word in Family	Place and Source I Saw, Heard, or Used It — classroom · school · home — conversation · book · TV · other	How It Was Used (sentence or phrase)	It Means . . . (as used in this specific context)
	First Time — Date: _____				
	Second Time — Date: _____				
	Third Time — Date: _____				

Hotshot Points _____

Levels of Achievement

Hotshot ☆ 40 points

Big Shot ☆ 30 points

Little Shot ☆ 20 points

NOTEBOOK POINT SYSTEM   Use interactive whiteboard technology to display the Vocabulary Hotshot Notebook Page. Point out that there is a separate fill-in entry form for each new word and that there are two forms on each notebook page. Then describe the notebook point system. Tell students that they get one point for accurately completing a First Time, Second Time, or Third Time row of requested information. They can earn three points for each word. In one week, at eight words per week, they can earn a total of 24 points. In two weeks, they can earn a total of 48 points. Out of the possible 48 points, they will need 40 points to become a Vocabulary Hotshot. Explain that the First Time row will be completed as a group in class when a new word is introduced, so that all students can easily earn at least 16 points.

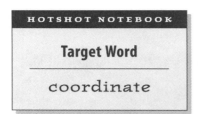

HOTSHOT NOTEBOOK

Target Word

coordinate

Teach/Model

Before Reading the Selection

Before reading an independently read text selection, introduce a target word by having students read and pronounce it. After repeating the word with you, students can record the word in their Vocabulary Hotshot Notebooks. For this sample lesson model, the word *coordinate* is used, a target word from the sample text "Alaska Adventure."

VOCABULARY WORD Continue displaying the Vocabulary Hotshot Notebook Page. Point to and read aloud the top line: Vocabulary Word. Tell students that you are going to print the new vocabulary word *coordinate* on the line labeled Vocabulary Word and that they should do the same.

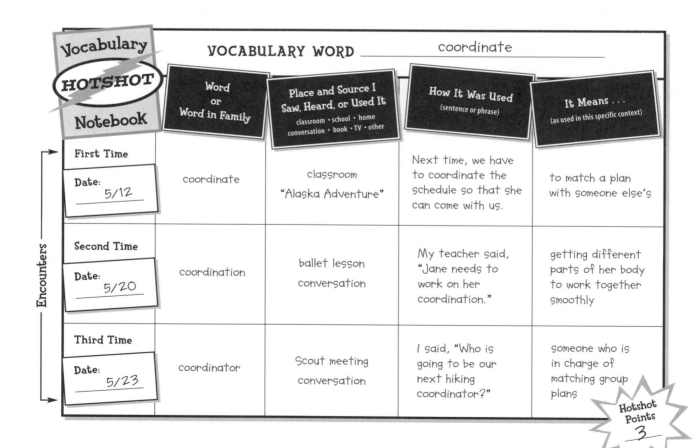

Vocabulary HOTSHOT Notebook

VOCABULARY WORD _____ coordinate _____

Encounters		Word or Word in Family	Place and Source I Saw, Heard, or Used It (classroom · school · home conversation · book · TV · other)	How It Was Used (sentence or phrase)	It Means . . . (as used in this specific context)
First Time	Date: 5/12	coordinate	classroom "Alaska Adventure"	Next time, we have to coordinate the schedule so that she can come with us.	to match a plan with someone else's
Second Time	Date: 5/20	coordination	ballet lesson conversation	My teacher said, "Jane needs to work on her coordination."	getting different parts of her body to work together smoothly
Third Time	Date: 5/23	coordinator	Scout meeting conversation	I said, "Who is going to be our next hiking coordinator?"	someone who is in charge of matching group plans

Hotshot Points 3

After Reading the Selection

COORDINATE
to match a plan with
someone else's

After providing a student-friendly explanation for *coordinate*, tell students that they will add to their Notebooks what they now know about the word. Point to and read aloud the first column: First Time and Date, Second Time and Date, and Third Time and Date. Explain to students that each entry form has a place for three encounters with the word or a word in the same family. Tell students that the First Time row is where they will record information about a new word introduced in class.

WORD OR WORD IN FAMILY Tell students that you are going to show them how to fill in the First Time row. Print today's date in the space labeled Date and then print the word *coordinate* in the first row of the column labeled Word or Word in Family. Have students do the same. Remind students that a group of words that has the same root word is called a word family and that words that belong to the same word family are related in meaning. Point out that the words *coordination, coordinated,* and *coordinator* all belong to the same word family as *coordinate*.

PLACE AND SOURCE I SAW, HEARD, OR USED IT Point to and read aloud the next column heading. Explain to students that in this column they will record the place they saw, heard, or used a word; for example, in class, in the school cafeteria, on the street, at home, or at a movie theater. They will also record the source; for example, a book, a magazine, a web page, a billboard, a TV show, a radio program, or a conversation. Tell them that for the word *coordinate,* the place they read it is in the classroom and the source is a selection called "Alaska Adventure." Print *classroom* and *"Alaska Adventure"* in the first row of the third column and have students do the same.

193

HOTSHOT NOTEBOOK

Target Word

coordinate

Next time, we have to **coordinate** the schedule so that she can come with us.

VARIATION Students can use the Vocabulary Hotshot Notebook to record words they discover on their own—words encountered in independent reading or words heard outside the classroom—that they find particularly fascinating or interesting.

HOW IT WAS USED Point to and read aloud the next column heading. Explain that this column is for recording the actual sentence or phrase in which the word was used. In "Alaska Adventure," *coordinate* was used in the following sentence: "Next time, we have to coordinate the schedule so that she can come with us." Tell students that in the first row of the fourth column you are going to write the sentence in which *coordinate* occurred and that they should do the same.

IT MEANS . . . Point to and read aloud the next column heading. Remind students that they have discussed the meaning of *coordinate* and that now they will explain the meaning in their own words. If they want to, students can use a dictionary to confirm their meaning. Then print "to match a plan with someone else's" in the first row of the fifth column and have students do the same.

Point to and read aloud Hotshot Points. Conclude by telling students that now they have filled in the whole First Time row and that for this they will each earn one point. Points will be counted every two weeks.

Extend Word Knowledge

Using an example such as the one shown above, display a completed entry for the word *coordinate*. Point out to students that for *coordinate* there are still two more rows to be filled in and that this is the real challenge. Tell students that the Second Time and Third Time rows are where they should record seeing, hearing, or using the word *coordinate,* or words related to *coordinate.* Explain that for second and third encounters students can also get points for practicing the word: using it either in conversation or in their written work. Emphasize that with many words, the meaning and the way it was used will differ on the second and third encounters, depending on the context in which the word was used. They cannot simply fill in the same information automatically for each encounter. Then go over the sample entries in the Second Time and Third Time rows, making sure that students understand the procedure.

References

Anderson, R. C. 1996. Research foundations to support wide reading. In V. Greany (ed.), *Promoting reading in developing countries*. Newark, DE: International Reading Association.

Anderson, R. C., and P. Freebody. 1981. Vocabulary knowledge. In J. Guthrie (ed.), *Comprehension and teaching research review* (pp. 77–117). Newark, DE: International Reading Association.

Anderson, R. C., and W. E. Nagy. 1992. The vocabulary conundrum. *American Educator* 16, pp. 14–18, 44–47.

Anderson, V., and M. Roit. 1998. Reading as a gateway to language proficiency for language-minority students in elementary grades. In R. M. Gersten and R. T. Jimenez (eds.), *Promoting learning for culturally and linguistically diverse students*. Belmont, CA: Wadsworth.

Anglin, J. M. 1993. Vocabulary development: A morphological analysis. *Monographs of the Society for Research in Child Development* 58 (Serial No. 238).

Armbruster, B., F. Lehr, and J. Osborn. 2001. *Put reading first: The research building blocks for teaching children to read*. Jessup, MD: National Institute for Literacy.

August, D., M. Carlo, C. Dressler, and C. Snow. 2005. The critical role of vocabulary development for English language learners. *Learning Disabilities: Research & Practice* 20(1), pp. 50–57.

Bannon, E., P. J. Fisher, L. Pozzi, and D. Wessel. 1990. Effective definitions for word learning. *Journal of Reading* 34.

Baumann, J. F., E. C. Edwards, E. M. Boland, S. Olejnik, and E. J. Kame'enui. 2003. Vocabulary tricks: Effects of instruction in morphology and context on fifth-grade students' ability to derive and infer word meanings. *American Educational Research Journal* 40(2), pp. 447–494.

Baumann, J. F., E. C. Edwards, G. Font, C. A. Tereshinski, E. J. Kame'enui, and S. Olejnik. 2002. Teaching morphemic and contextual analysis to fifth-grade students. *Reading Research Quarterly* 37(2), pp. 150–176.

Baumann, J. F., G. Font, E. C. Edwards, and E. Boland. 2005. Strategies for teaching middle-grade students to use word-part and context clues. In E. H. Hiebert and M. L. Kamil (eds.), *Teaching and learning vocabulary: Bringing research to practice*. Mahwah, NJ: Erlbaum.

Bear, D. R., M. Invernizzi, S. Templeton, and F. Johnston. 1996. *Words their way: Word study for phonics, vocabulary, and spelling instruction*. Upper Saddle River, NJ: Prentice-Hall.

Beck, I. L., and M. G. McKeown. 1985. Teaching vocabulary: Making the instruction fit the goal. *Educational Perspectives* 23(1), pp. 11–15.

Beck, I. L., and M. G. McKeown. 2001. Text talk: Capturing the benefits of read-aloud experiences for young children. *Reading Teacher* 55, pp. 10–20.

Beck, I. L., M. G. McKeown, and L. Kucan. 2002. *Bringing words to life: Robust vocabulary instruction*. New York: Guilford.

Beck, I. L., C. Perfetti, and M. G. McKeown. 1982. The effects of long-term vocabulary instruction on lexical access and reading comprehension. *Journal of Educational Psychology* 74.

Biemiller, A. 1999. *Language and reading success*. Brookline, MA: Brookline Books.

Biemiller. A. 2003. Vocabulary: Needed if more children are to read well. *Reading Psychology* 24, pp. 323–335.

Biemiller. A. 2004. Teaching vocabulary in the primary grades. In J. F. Baumann and E. J. Kame'enui (eds.), *Vocabulary instruction: Research to practice*. New York: Guilford.

Biemiller, A. 2005a. Size and sequence in vocabulary development: Implications for choosing words for primary grade vocabulary instruction. In E. H. Hiebert and M. L. Kamil (eds.), *Teaching and learning vocabulary: Bringing research to practice.* Mahwah, NJ: Erlbaum.

Biemiller, A. 2005b. Vocabulary development and instruction: A prerequisite for school learning. In D. Dickinson and S. Neuman (eds.), *Handbook of early literacy research,* Vol. 2. New York: Guilford.

Biemiller, A., and C. Boote. 2006. An effective method for building meaning vocabulary in primary grades. *Journal of Educational Psychology* 98(1), pp. 42–62.

Biemiller, A., and M. Slonim. 2001. Estimating root word vocabulary growth in normative and advantaged populations: Evidence for a common sequence of vocabulary acquisition. *Journal of Educational Psychology* 93(3), pp. 438–520.

Blachowicz, C., and P. Fisher. 2002. *Teaching vocabulary in all classrooms* (2nd ed.). Upper Saddle River, NJ: Merrill/Prentice-Hall.

Blachowicz, C., and P. Fisher. 2004. Keep the "fun" in fundamental: Encouraging word awareness and incidental word learning in the classroom through word play. In J. F. Baumann and E. J. Kame'enui (eds.), *Vocabulary instruction: Research to practice.* New York: Guilford.

Bravo, M. A., E. H. Hiebert, and P. D. Pearson. 2005. Tapping the linguistic resources of Spanish/English bilinguals: The role of cognates in science. Berkeley: Lawrence Hall of Science, University of California.

Calderón, M., D. August, R. Slavin, D. Duran, N. Madden, and A. Cheung. 2005. Bring words to life in classrooms with English-language learners. In E. H. Hiebert and M. L. Kamil (eds.), *Teaching and learning vocabulary: Bringing research to practice.* Mahwah, NJ: Erlbaum.

Carlo, M., D. August, B. McLaughlin, C. Snow, C. Dressler, D. Lipman, T. Lively, and C. White. 2004. Closing the gap: Addressing the vocabulary needs of English language learners in bilingual and mainstream classrooms. *Reading Research Quarterly* 40.

Carroll, J. B., P. Davies, and B. Richman. 1971. *The American Heritage word frequency book.* Boston: Houghton Mifflin.

Chall, J., and E. Dale 1995. *Readability revisited: The new Dale-Chall readability formula.* Brookline, MA: Brookline Books.

Coyne, M. D., D. Simmons, and E. J. Kame'enui. 2004. Vocabulary instruction for young children at risk of experiencing reading difficulties: Teaching word meanings during shared story reading. In J. F. Baumann and E. J. Kame'enui (eds.), *Vocabulary instruction: Research to practice.* New York: Guilford.

Cunningham, A. E. 2005. Vocabulary growth through independent reading and reading aloud to children. In E. H. Hiebert and M. L. Kamil (eds.), *Teaching and learning vocabulary: Bringing research to practice.* Mahwah, NJ: Erlbaum.

Cunningham, A. E., and K. E. Stanovich. 1997. Early reading acquisition and its relation to reading experience and ability 10 years later. *Developmental Psychology* 33(6), pp. 934–945.

Cunningham, A. E., and K. E. Stanovich. 1998. What reading does for the mind. *American Educator* 22, pp. 8–15.

Curtis, M. E., and R. Glaser. 1983. Reading theory and the assessment of reading achievement. *Journal of Educational Measurement* 20, pp. 133–147.

Dale, E. 1965. Vocabulary measurement: Techniques and major findings. *Elementary English* 42, pp. 82–88.

Dale, E., and J. O'Rourke. 1981. *Living word vocabulary.* Chicago: World Book/Childcraft International.

Dressler, C. 2000. The word-inferencing strategies of bilingual and monolingual fifth graders: A case study approach. Unpublished qualifying paper, Harvard Graduate School of Education, Cambridge, MA.

Edwards, E. C., G. Font, J. F. Baumann, and E. Boland. 2004. Unlocking word meanings: Strategies and guidelines for teaching morphemic and contextual analysis. In J. F. Baumann and E. J. Kame'enui (eds.), *Vocabulary instruction: Research to practice.* New York: Guilford.

Foorman, B. R., D. J. Francis, S. E. Shaywitz, B. A. Shaywitz, and J. M. Fletcher. 1997. The case for early reading intervention. In B. A. Blachman (ed.), *Foundations of reading acquisition and dyslexia: Implications for early intervention.* Mahwah, NJ: Erlbaum.

Fukkink, R. G., and K. de Glopper. 1998. Effects of instruction in deriving word meaning from context: A meta-analysis. *Review of Educational Research* 68, pp. 450–469.

Gersten, R., and S. Baker. 2001. *Topical summary: Practices for English-language learners.* Eugene, OR: National Institute for Urban School Improvement.

Graves, M. F. 2000. A vocabulary program to complement and bolster a middle-grade comprehension program. In B. M. Taylor, M. F. Graves, and P. Van Den Broek (eds.), *Reading for meaning: Fostering comprehension in the middle grades.* New York: Teachers College Press.

Graves, M. F. 2004. Teaching prefixes: As good as it gets? In J. F. Baumann and E. J. Kame'enui (eds.), *Vocabulary instruction: Research to practice.* New York: Guilford.

Graves, M. F., C. Juel, and B. B. Graves. 2004. *Teaching reading in the twenty-first century* (3rd ed.). Boston: Allyn & Bacon.

196

Graves, M. F., and S. M. Watts-Taffe. 2002. The place of word consciousness in a research-based vocabulary program. In A. E. Farstrup and S. J. Samuels (eds.), *What research has to say about reading instruction*. Newark, DE: International Reading Association.

Hart, B., and T. R. Risley. 1995. *Meaningful differences in the everyday experience of young American children*. Baltimore, MD: Paul H. Brookes.

Hayes, D. P., L. T. Wolfer, and M. F. Wolfe. 1996. Schoolbook simplification and its relation to the decline in SAT-verbal scores. *American Educational Research Journal 33*, pp. 489–508.

Henry, M. K. 1997. The decoding/spelling continuum: Integrated decoding and spelling instruction from pre-school to early secondary school. *Dyslexia 3*.

Henry, M. K. 2003. *Unlocking literacy: Effective decoding & spelling instruction*. Baltimore, MD: Paul H. Brookes.

Jenkins, J. R., and R. Dixon. 1983. Vocabulary learning. *Contemporary Educational Psychology 8*, pp. 237–280.

Johnson, D. D. 2001. *Vocabulary in the elementary and middle school*. Boston: Allyn & Bacon.

Johnson, D. D., B. von H. Johnson, and K. Schlichting. 2004. Logology: Word and language play. In J. F. Baumann and E. J. Kame'enui (eds.), *Vocabulary instruction: Research to practice*. New York: Guilford.

Kamil, M. L. 2004. Vocabulary and comprehension instruction: Summary and implications of the National Reading Panel finding. In P. McCardle and V. Chhabra (eds.), *The voice of evidence in reading research*. Baltimore, MD: Paul H. Brookes.

Kamil, M. L., and E. H. Hiebert. 2005. Teaching and learning vocabulary: Perspectives and persistent issues. In E. H. Hiebert and M. L. Kamil (eds.), *Teaching and learning vocabulary: Bringing research to practice*. Mahwah, NJ: Erlbaum.

Kuhn, M. R., and S. A. Stahl. 1998. Teaching children to learn word meanings from context: A synthesis and some questions. *Journal of Literacy Research 30*, pp. 119–138.

Lane, H.B., and S. A. Allen. 2010. The vocabulary-rich classroom: Modeling sophisticated word use to promote word consciousness and vocabulary growth. *Reading Teacher 63(5)*, pp. 362–370.

Mastropieri, M. A., and T. E. Scruggs. 1998. Enhancing school success with mnemonic strategies. *Intervention in School and Clinic,* March 1998.

McKeown, M. G., and I. Beck. 2004. Direct and rich vocabulary instruction. In J. F. Baumann and E. J. Kame'enui (eds.), *Vocabulary instruction: Research to practice*. New York: Guilford.

McKeown, M. G., I. L. Beck, R. C. Omanson, and M. T. Pople. 1985. Some effects of the nature and frequency of vocabulary instruction on the knowledge and use of words. *Reading Research Quarterly 20*, pp. 522–535.

Miller, G., and P. Gildea. 1987. How children learn words. *Scientific American 27*, pp. 94–99.

Moffett, J., and B. J. Wagner. 1992. *Student-centered language arts: K–12* (4th ed.). Portsmouth, NH: Heinemann.

Nagy, W. E. 1988. *Teaching vocabulary to improve reading comprehension*. Newark, DE: International Reading Association.

Nagy, W. E. 2005. Why vocabulary instruction needs to be long-term and comprehensive. In E. H. Hiebert and M. L. Kamil (eds.), *Teaching and learning vocabulary: Bringing research to practice*. Mahwah, NJ: Erlbaum.

Nagy, W. E., and R. C. Anderson. 1984. How many words are there in printed school English? *Reading Research Quarterly 19*, pp. 304–330.

Nagy, W. E., R. C. Anderson, and P. A. Herman. 1987. Learning word meanings from context during normal reading. *American Educational Research Journal 24*, pp. 237–270.

Nagy, W. E., R. C. Anderson, M. Schommer, J. A. Scott, and A. Stallman. 1989. Morphological families in the internal lexicon. *Reading Research Quarterly 24*, pp. 262–282.

Nagy, W. E., I. N. Diakidoy, and R. C. Anderson. 1993. The acquisition of morphology: Learning the contribution of suffixes to the meanings of derivatives. *Journal of Reading Behavior 25*, pp. 155–170.

Nagy, W. E., G. E. Garcia, A.Y. Durgunoglu, and B. Hancin-Bhatt. 1993. Spanish-English bilingual students' use of cognates in English reading. *Journal of Reading Behavior 25*, pp. 241–259.

Nagy, W. E., P. A. Herman, and R. C. Anderson. 1985. Learning words from context. *Reading Research Quarterly 20*, pp. 233–253.

Nagy, W. E., and J. A. Scott. 2000. Vocabulary processes. In M. L. Kamil, P. Mosenthal, P. D. Pearson, and R. Barr (eds.), *Handbook of reading research*, Vol. 3. Mahwah, NJ: Erlbaum.

National Center for Educational Statistics. 2005. *The condition of education*. Washington, DC: U.S. Department of Education.

197

National Reading Panel. 2000. *Teaching children to read: An evidence-based assessment of the scientific research literature on reading and its implications for reading instruction.* Washington, DC: National Institute of Child Health and Human Development.

Readence, J. 2004. Semantic feature analysis. *Nevada Reading First Newsletter* 1(4).

Rodriguez, T. A. 2001. From the known to the unknown: Using cognates to teach English- and Spanish-speaking literates. *Reading Teacher* 54(8), pp. 744–746.

Schwartz, R. M., and T. E. Raphael. 1985. Concept of definition: A key to improving students' vocabulary. *Reading Teacher* 39, pp. 198–203.

Scott, J. A. 2005. Creating opportunities to acquire new word meanings from text. In E. H. Hiebert and M. L. Kamil (eds.), *Teaching and learning vocabulary: Bringing research to practice.* Mahwah, NJ: Erlbaum.

Scott, J. A., and W. E. Nagy. 1997. Understanding the definitions of unfamiliar verbs. *Reading Research Quarterly* 32, pp. 184–200.

Scott, J. A., and W. E. Nagy. 2004. Developing word consciousness. In J. F. Baumann and E. J. Kame'enui (eds.), *Vocabulary instruction: Research to practice.* New York: Guilford.

Stahl, S. A. 1999. *Vocabulary development.* Brookline, MA: Brookline Books.

Stahl, S. A. 2005. Four problems with teaching word meanings (and what to do to make vocabulary an integral part of instruction). In E. H. Hiebert and M. L. Kamil (eds.), *Teaching and learning vocabulary: Bringing research to practice.* Mahwah, NJ: Erlbaum.

Stahl, S. A., and C. H. Clark. 1987. The effects of participatory expectations in classroom discussion on learning of science vocabulary. *American Educational Research Journal* 24, pp. 541–556.

Stahl, S. A., and M. Fairbanks. 1986. The effects of vocabulary instruction: A model-based meta-analysis. *Review of Educational Research* 5.

Stahl, S. A., and B. A. Kapinus. 1991. Possible sentences: Predicting word meanings to teach content area vocabulary. *Reading Teacher* 45, pp. 36–38.

Stahl, S. A., and B. A. Kapinus. 2001. *Word power: What every educator needs to know about teaching vocabulary.* Washington, DC: National Education Association.

Stahl, S. A., and W. E. Nagy. 2000. *Promoting vocabulary development.* Austin: Texas Education Agency.

Sternberg, R. J. 1987. Most words are learned from context. In M. G. McKeown and M. E. Curtis (eds.), *The acquisition of word meanings.* Mahwah, NJ: Erlbaum.

Swanborn, M. S., and K. de Glopper. 1999. Incidental word learning while reading: A meta-analysis. *Review of Educational Research* 69, pp. 261–285.

Templeton, S. 1997. *Teaching the integrated language arts.* Boston: Houghton Mifflin.

White, T. J., M. A. Power, and S. White. 1989. Morphological analysis: Implications for teaching and understanding vocabulary growth. *Reading Research Quarterly* 24, pp. 283–304.

White, T. G., J. Sowell, and A. Yanagihara. 1989. Teaching elementary students to use word-part clues. *Reading Teacher* 42, pp. 302–308.

198

C O N N E C T

T O   T H E O R Y

Answer Key . . .

PAGE 85

English/Spanish Cognates in "Marine Mammals"

animals/animales
marine/marino
ocean/océano
impossible/imposible
air/aire
creature/criatura
comparison/comparación
impulse/impulso
react/reaccionar

number/número
group/grupo
filters/filtros
material/material
giants/gigantes
abundant/abundante
planet/planeta
population/población
protect/proteger

False English/Spanish Cognate in "Marine Mammals"

miles/miles (In Spanish, *miles* means "thousands.")

PAGE 165

Layers of the English Language

Anglo-Saxon: table, made, branch, book, airplane, after

Latin: respectful, predict, pedestrian, instructor, export, audit, omit

Greek: telephoto, phonogram, micrometer, geocentric, grapheme, astrology

VOCABULARY HANDBOOK

Resources

specific
word
instruction
word-learning
strategies
word
consciousness

For printable PDFs of the Resources section, go to www.brookespublishing.com/diamond/materials

Contents		Page
Sample Texts	Alaska Adventure	201
	Common Sense: An Anansi Tale	202
	Marine Mammals	204
	Percussion Instruments	205
	Studying the Sky	206
	Weekend Campout	207
Activity Masters	Concept of Definition Map	208
	Five-Senses Simile Web	209
	PAVE Map	210
	Vocabulary Hotshot Notebook Page	211
	The Vocabulary Strategy Worksheet	212
	Word Map	213
	Word-Part Web	214
Teaching Charts	Types of Helpful Context Clues	215
	The Vocabulary Strategy	216
	Where Is the Fly?	217

Alaska Adventure

J ake Mays and his dad spent two weeks visiting Alaska. They flew to Anchorage and then took a train south to a lodge in Seward, a small harbor town surrounded by the Kenai mountain range. From there they took day trips around the area to see and experience the sights. Jake found it all so enticing that he never wanted to leave.

Every day brought a new adventure. They traveled by ferry and sailboat on the marine highways through straits and inlets. They paddled sea kayaks up narrow fjords lined with ice cliffs. They saw whales, otters, puffins, sea lions, and eagles. They spent a day on a fishing schooner catching salmon for dinner. Jake snapped pictures of every new vista.

"Mom is not going to believe how awesome the scenery is," he said. "Next time, we have to coordinate the schedule so that she can come with us."

On the flight home, they pored over the map, already planning the return trip. Jake thought it would be exciting to do some backpacking on Mount McKinley, the tallest peak in North America.

"Wouldn't it be fun to explore the state's interior? We could travel north from Anchorage to visit Denali National Park. I heard that the fishing is first class, and there is plenty of wildlife to see."

"That's true," said Dad. "Still, it is hard to resist the idea of retracing the route we just traveled. Now that we're expert kayakers, we should paddle around the capes and coves and lagoons of the Alaska Peninsula." Dad pointed at the chain of volcanic islands separating the Pacific Ocean from the Bering Sea. "The Aleutian archipelago stretches for more than a thousand miles. We could spend a lifetime on the water just exploring this part of the Ring of Fire."

"Well, that settles it," said Jake. "We just need to come back and stay longer."

"You've got that right," said Dad.

Common Sense: An Anansi Tale

ANANSI, THE SPIDER, was full of mischief. He loved to play jokes and pull pranks on people. One day, he decided to collect all the common sense in the world. Everyone uses these little bits of good judgment every day. "If," Anansi thought, "I alone had all of this sensible information, I could sell it back to people when they needed it." Anansi imagined people lining up to pay him for answers to the simplest questions: *Anansi, what should I wear when it's cold outside? What should I do when I am hungry?*

"This is a brilliant scheme," thought Anansi. "I will have all the common sense in the world, and all the money in the world, too!"

So Anansi got a sack and started collecting common sense. *Brush your teeth to prevent cavities! Put your socks on before your shoes!* Anansi put them all in his sack.

The sack was soon bursting at the seams. "I need to find a better place to keep the common sense," thought Anansi. Just then he spied a calabash growing on a vine. It looked like a giant pumpkin. Anansi hollowed out the calabash. Then he stuffed all of the common sense inside and kept collecting.

When Anansi had gathered up every bit of common sense, he thought, "Now I just have to find a good place to hide it."

Anansi set off through the jungle to find just the right hiding place. He dragged the calabash under ferns and over logs. He waded through streams. He trudged from shrub to bush to hedge. He hiked up muddy trails and slid down steep hillsides. Finally Anansi found the tallest tree in the jungle.

"This is the perfect hiding place," he said. "The calabash will be safe and sound. No one would ever guess that I have hidden such a valuable treasure in such an unusual place."

Using a thick rope, Anansi tied the heavy calabash around his neck so that it dangled in front of him like a locket on a necklace. He started up the tree trunk, but climbing was hard. The calabash flopped and swayed. It banged Anansi's belly. It bruised his knees and elbows. The rope burned the back of his neck. But even though Anansi was aching and battered, he did not stop. The thought of getting rich kept him going.

As Anansi was struggling upward, he heard someone giggling below him. He looked down and saw a small boy leaning against the tree trunk.

Anansi called down to the boy. "What is so funny?" he asked.

"*You* are," said the boy. "Anyone with a pinch of common sense knows that it is easier to carry things on your back—especially if you are climbing a tree. How foolish can you get?"

The boy's words made Anansi furious! Anansi thought he had collected all the common sense in the world. How could he have missed the one piece he needed most? The thought made Anansi madder and madder. Finally he lost his temper and swung the calabash with all his might against the tree trunk.

The calabash shattered into a million pieces. The common sense spilled out and pieces got caught in a breeze. The breeze blew little pieces of common sense all over the world. And that explains why today everyone has a little bit of common sense to use and a little bit of common sense to share. But, as you yourself know, nobody got all of it. It was Anansi who made it happen that way.

Marine Mammals

MAMMALS ARE WARM-BLOODED ANIMALS. Marine mammals, such as whales, live in the ocean. Unlike fish, marine mammals cannot breathe underwater. They can dive very deep to find food. They can stay under the water for a long time. However, it is impossible for them to stay below the surface for an indefinite amount of time. They regularly need to resurface to get air.

One marine mammal is the largest animal ever to be found on Earth. This huge creature, called a blue whale, can be 90 feet long. It can weigh more than 100 tons. The blue whale is also the loudest animal on earth. It makes a deep, resounding rumble that has no comparison on land or sea. Whenever the blue whale has the impulse to talk to other whales, it sends out a noise that travels uninterrupted through the ocean. Other whales react when they hear the call even if they are many miles away.

The blue whale requires an unusual amount of food each day. You might think that it hunts big game in the sea, but you would be incorrect. It lives on an infinite number of extremely tiny creatures. They are called krill. With its mouth gaping wide, the whale swims into a school, or group, of krill. The whale scoops up the krill, along with a big mouthful of seawater. In place of teeth, the whale has rows of fringe-like filters called baleen. Baleen is made of material that looks like stiff bristles or hairs. It acts like a strainer. It lets the seawater flow out of the whale's mouth but traps the krill.

Blue whales may be mighty giants, but they are endangered. Though once they were abundant, today very few blue whales remain on our planet. Overhunting caused an imbalance in their population. New laws help to protect them and increase their numbers. We should be grateful for the caring people who have united, with a goal of ensuring the survival of these wonderful creatures.

Percussion Instruments

From primitive cave dwellers to modern city dwellers, people have always played percussion instruments. A percussion instrument is any musical instrument that you play by striking or hitting using either sticks or your hands. There are many kinds of percussion instruments, including drums, cymbals, and xylophones.

Of all the percussion instruments, drums are the most prevalent. They are commonly found all over the world. Every culture has developed its own type of drum. The drums may differ from culture to culture, place to place, and group to group, but all of them possess the same basic elements. They usually have a hollow shell, or frame, and a round drumhead.

The shell can come in many shapes and sizes. Shells are usually made out of metal or wood. They can be shallow like a snare drum's or deep like a conga drum's. They can be shaped like a cereal bowl, an hourglass, or even a kettle. The shell acts like a speaker to amplify the sound, or make it louder. A small drum, like a bongo, will sound faint compared to the huge noise made by a big bass drum used in a marching band.

The drumhead is usually made from an animal hide. The animal hide, or skin, is stretched tight over the drum shell. When the drummer hits the drumhead, it vibrates, or moves very quickly back and forth. This vibration creates a resonant, or deep and rich, sound. A drum's pitch depends on the size and the tightness of the drumhead. A smaller, tighter drumhead makes a higher-pitched sound.

Drumbeats are like beating hearts. You can hear their rhythms through the ages.

Studying the Sky

STRONOMY is the study of the planets, stars, and galaxies. People have been watching the movement of the sun, moon, planets, and stars since ancient times. So astronomy is a very, very old science.

From early times, people tried to make models of the universe. For many years, no one wanted to believe that the sun was the center of the solar system. It took a long time for people to accept this heliocentric model, with the earth orbiting around the sun with the other planets.

It is interesting to study the night sky like the astronomers from centuries ago. You can see even the most distant stars with your eyes alone. And you may be able to identify constellations, or groups of stars. Constellations make pictures in the sky, such as Canis Major (the Great Dog) or Ursa Minor (the Little Bear).

A telescope can be used to see faraway things more clearly. With a telescope, you can see details like the craters of the moon and other features of the lunar landscape, the moons of Jupiter, and the rings of Saturn.

Astronomy is like taking a trip back in time. This evening you can look at the same planets and stars that ancient astronomers observed so long ago.

Weekend Campout

THE FRANCO FAMILY loves to be outdoors. They spend almost every weekend camping. Fay Franco adores camping more than anything. She will even pitch her tent in the backyard just to sleep outside.

Fay has been to lots of campgrounds. Mar Vista Shores is her favorite. The campsites are in the tall trees. Each spot has a beach view.

At Mar Vista Shores, noisy birdcalls wake Fay early. She hears loud squawking and jumps up for breakfast. Then she packs a picnic. Fay and her dad drive to the trailhead. It is the place where the hiking trails start. They choose a path to take. Dad carries a daypack. It holds a first aid kit, sweatshirts, food, and water. The path leads sharply uphill to a waterfall. It is a steep climb! They hungrily devour their lunch by the riverbank. From the rocks, Fay can watch the water plummet over the cliff.

In the afternoon, Fay and her mom go to the seashore. Mom is a rock hound. She hunts for neat-looking stones. Fay makes sandcastles. Using wet sand, she builds high walls and towers. Sometimes she pokes around the tide pools. She looks for crabs and starfish in the rocks along the beach.

At dinnertime, the Franco family usually has a sunset cookout. They light a campfire. They roast hotdogs. The sky turns pink over the water. Nighttime falls. Fay gets into her sleeping bag. She looks up to see the stars twinkle overhead.

Fay thinks that weekend campouts are almost perfect. The only flaw comes when it is time to go home.

CONCEPT OF DEFINITION MAP

What Is It Like?

What Is It?

What Are Some Examples?

FIVE-SENSES SIMILE WEB

feels like . . .

tastes like . . .

sounds like . . .

smells like . . .

looks like . . .

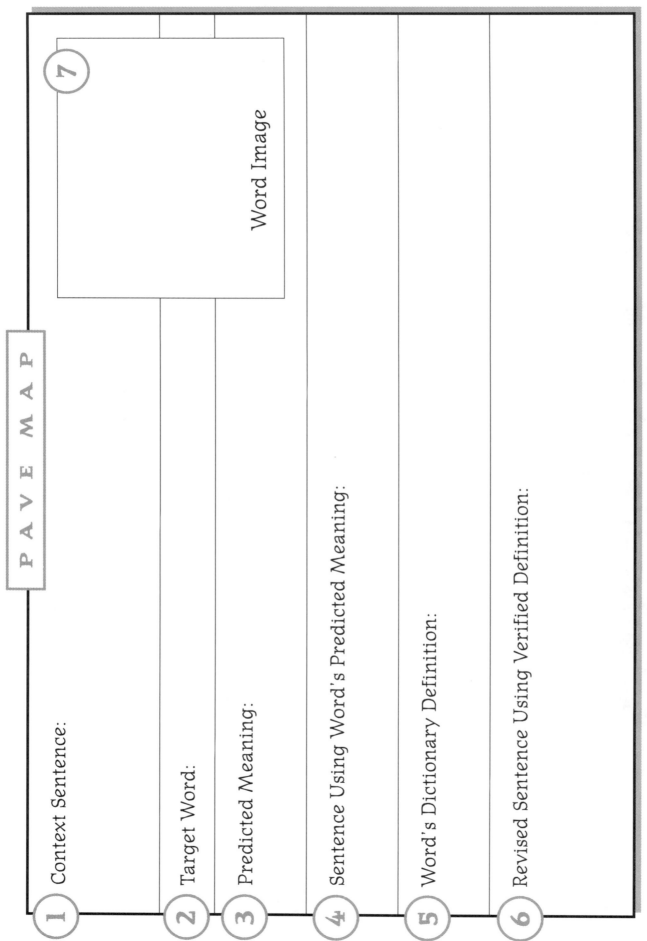

P A V E M A P

7 Word Image

1 Context Sentence:

2 Target Word:

3 Predicted Meaning:

4 Sentence Using Word's Predicted Meaning:

5 Word's Dictionary Definition:

6 Revised Sentence Using Verified Definition:

Vocabulary HOTSHOT Notebook

VOCABULARY WORD _____

Encounters		Word or Word in Family	Place and Source I Saw, Heard, or Used It classroom • school • home conversation • book • TV • other	How It Was Used (sentence or phrase)	It Means . . . (as used in this specific context)
	First Time Date: _____				
	Second Time Date: _____				
	Third Time Date: _____				

Hotshot Points _____

Vocabulary HOTSHOT Notebook

VOCABULARY WORD _____

Encounters		Word or Word in Family	Place and Source I Saw, Heard, or Used It classroom • school • home conversation • book • TV • other	How It Was Used (sentence or phrase)	It Means . . . (as used in this specific context)
	First Time Date: _____				
	Second Time Date: _____				
	Third Time Date: _____				

Hotshot Points _____

The Vocabulary Strategy Worksheet

Context Sentence(s) _____

_____

_____

1 Look for Context Clues

Context Clues	Signal Words or Punctuation	Type of Context Clue

2 Look for Word-Part Clues

A. Word Broken into Parts

A. Can You Break the Word into Parts? Circle **yes** or **no**.
(If you can't, skip to Step 3.)

	Word Part	Meaning
B. What Is the Root Word?		
C. What Is the Prefix?		
D. What Is the Suffix?		
E. Put the Meanings of the Word Parts Together		

Prefix + Root Word • Root Word + Suffix • Prefix + Root Word + Suffix

3 I Guess the Word Means . . .

4 My Meaning Substituted in the Original Sentence

Does your meaning make sense in the sentence? Circle **yes** or **no**.

5 Dictionary Says . . .

Was your meaning close to the dictionary definition? Circle **yes** or **no**.

WORD MAP

ANTONYM

SYNONYM

NONEXAMPLE

EXAMPLE

WORD-PART WEB

TYPES OF HELPFUL CONTEXT CLUES

Type	Description	Example Sentence
Definition	The author provides a direct definition of an unfamiliar word, right in the sentence. • SIGNAL WORDS: *is, are, means, refers to*	A conga *is* a barrel-shaped drum.
Appositive Definition	A type of definition clue. An appositive is a word or phrase that defines or explains an unfamiliar word that comes before it. • SIGNAL WORD: *or* • SIGNAL PUNCTUATION: set off by commas	At night you can see constellations, *or* groups of stars, in the sky.
Synonym	The author uses another word or phrase that is similar in meaning, or can be compared, to an unfamiliar word. • SIGNAL WORDS: *also, as, identical, like, likewise, resembling, same, similarly, too*	My dog Buck travels everywhere with me. My friend's canine buddy travels everywhere with him, *too*.
Antonym	The author uses another word or phrase that means about the opposite of, or is in contrast with, an unfamiliar word. • SIGNAL WORDS: *but, however, in contrast, instead of, on the other hand, though, unlike*	I thought the movie would be weird, *but* it turned out to be totally mundane.
Example	The author provides several words or ideas that are examples of an unfamiliar word. • SIGNAL WORDS: *for example, for instance, including, like, such as*	In science we are studying marine mammals *such as* whales, dolphins, and porpoises.
General	The author provides some nonspecific clues to the meaning of an unfamiliar word, often spread over several sentences.	Einstein rode his bike everywhere. He thought driving a car was way too complicated.

THE VOCABULARY STRATEGY

To figure out the meaning of an unfamiliar word that you come across while reading:

1. **Look for Context Clues** in the Words, Phrases, and Sentences Surrounding the Unfamiliar Word

2. **Look for Word–Part Clues** Within the Unfamiliar Word
   A. Try to Break the Word into Parts. (If you can't, skip to Step 3.)
   B. Look at the Root Word. What does it mean?
   C. Look at the Prefix. What does it mean?
   D. Look at the Suffix. What does it mean?
   E. Put the Meanings of the Word Parts Together. What is the meaning of the whole word?

3. **Guess the Word's Meaning** (Use Steps 1 and 2.)

4. **Try Out Your Meaning in the Original Sentence** to Check Whether or Not It Makes Sense in Context

5. **Use the Dictionary**, if Necessary, to Confirm Your Meaning

Where Is the Fly?

INDEX

Page references in italics refer to charts, graphic organizers, and resources.